ALBRECHT AND FARROW ON GUNS

LIVING THE CONCEALED CARRY LIFESTYLE

STEVE ALBRECHT AND MICHAEL FARROW

Dr. Steve Albrecht
PO Box 3092
Monument, CO 80132
DrSteve@DrSteveAlbrecht.com
www.DrSteveAlbrecht.com

Cover Photo by Jessica Archibald

Publishing Coordinator – Sharon Kizziah-Holmes

Paperback-Press
an imprint of A & S Publishing
Paperback Press, LLC
Springfield, Missouri

ISBN -13: 978-1-960499-90-5

Steve Albrecht Dedication

To Carly, a peaceful warrior in many ways.

Michael Farrow Dedication

I am constantly reminded that through properly-purposed planning and training, when faced with a serious situation, the best outcome will side with the most prepared. For those who take on the Concealed Carry lifestyle to protect themselves and others from harm, this book is in support of your courage to be properly prepared and ready. It's for the few sheepdogs in life that are willing stand up against a threat that ultimately protect the flocks.

CONTENTS

Steve Albrecht Acknowledgments

To Mike Farrow, always my tactical mentor and workplace violence prevention brainstorming partner.

Michael Farrow Acknowledgments

First and foremost, I owe a great debt of appreciation and thanks to my co-writer Dr. Steve Albrecht, whom I have worked with and shared worries for over three decades. Steve and I have addressed targeted violence in most every form and without hesitation, Steve has never swayed from the course of helping others. I am always inspired when working with Steve and especially on this project as part of the greater cause of being prepared through awareness and training, so we can ultimately save more lives.

Others have played a key role in my efforts to help recognize and disrupt targeted violence. My shooting training partner and co-instructor is Rick Levesque. Rick is relentless in finding ways to improve our practical shooting methods and especially since we are both much more senior in our age and abilities. Doug Farber, who has teamed with me over the years in developing properly-purposed protective intelligence and services approaches. Together, Doug and I created security models that consider the operational space and the means and methods targeted violence could impact the safety of people, property, and processes. It's when this approach is applied to the Concealed Carry Lifestyle, we can get ahead of the possible threat situation and find alternative methods to decrease or stop the threat before having to use our weapons.

A special thanks to my daughter-in-law Roya Farrow, who as a high school teacher found significant patience to help edit and provide better flow to my chapters. Besides being a wonderful addition to our family her patience and support was greatly appreciated.

Last but definitely not the least my wife, Staria. She has endured over three decades of my travels, work assignments, and long absences as I worked to help others. She has also lived the Concealed Carry Lifestyle and clearly understands it's not without its sacrifices to be prepared and ready for situations that we hope may never occur.

"The hardest thing to get people to understand in class: You literally have seconds to win a gunfight in a defensive shooting. If you are trying to shoot tight shot groups you need to open that shit up and shoot faster. Speed does count in a gunfight." – Michael Keyes

Army Special Ops and Infantry Vet, 3/75 Army Ranger
(Twitter @MichaelKeyes)

INTRODUCTION

Here's the bad news: The cops won't always be there to save you.

There will never be enough cops to come to your rescue and they can't always get to you fast enough anyway. Their numbers are either dwindling or staying the same, while crime goes up (slowly, but up nonetheless). There has not been a significant increase in the total number of police officers in several decades. Depending on which labor study you've seen, the number of US cops seems to range (wildly) from 750,000 to 900,000. That sounds like a lot of armed bodies in the field but it really isn't. (Why no one in the US government seems to be able to come up with an accurate figure is baffling. Why are we not surprised by that?)

If, as we often hear, that the number of police departments with 10 or fewer cops is around 48% of the total, and you live in one of those small cities or towns where that is true, there could only be one or two cops on duty in your neighborhood in any eight to twelve-hour period. Even in major cities, between sick days, training, vacation, court, and special assignments, there just aren't as many as cops around as you might want to believe. Las Vegas has 8 to 12 cops on The Strip on a normal day. San Diego has about 100 patrol cops on duty on each ten-hour shift, to protect the 1.4 million people who live in the eighth-largest city in the US. You get the idea: there seem to be more bad guys (2.3 million in our prisons, jails, and juvenile corrections facilities) than good guys out there.

The phrase "We're at minimum staffing tonight," is so

common at many police patrol divisions that the weary and shorthanded cops just smile and go about their business anyway. While we wouldn't operate a commercial passenger jet or a nuclear power plant or a professional baseball team at "minimum staffing," it seems perfectly acceptable to send our cops out into the morning or the night hopeful that if they have to ask for a cover unit, one will arrive before it no longer matters.

According to the staffing reports on private security guards in the US, we are relying and will continue to rely more and more on the 1.1 million private security officers to protect us at the airport, the mall, the hospital, the bank, and the parking lot and the lobby of the building where you may work.

Does this give you much comfort, that your life and safety from crime comes from somebody making at or barely-above the minimum wage? Many of these folks are probably nice people but unlike a cop, they are not paid to take a bullet for you or even get near to the side of the edge of the front of harm's way. This is not to attack security guards, some of whom are professional, skilled, and smart. But too many of them are lazy, fearful, undereducated, underpaid, and just trying to get through their work shift without having to do any real or confrontational work. A security colleague we know puts it even less delicately: "Sometimes we are protected ***by*** people we should be protected ***from.***"

There are no national licensing requirements or standards for security guard training or licensing in the U.S. There are no national standards or regulations for security officers to carry guns. This means the rules for important issues like powers of arrest, observing versus intervening, or carrying an exposed or concealed firearm while working, varies from state to state. The uniform-wearing, gun-toting guy or gal you see at a concert, outside the jewelry store, or arriving at your home to answer an alarm call from the security company hired by your homeowners' association who monitors the ringer, may have absolutely zero knowledge of how real crooks operate. Based on their lack of range time, some of them would be better off using their gun like a hammer, and try to batter their way to survival.

The point to these anecdotal statistic lessons is simple: When it comes to fighting crime in your neighborhood, it's going to bc up to you.

When a true threat to your life appears, sometime between tomorrow and twenty years from now, you will fail if you are not already prepared to win. You get that way through training, experience, role-playing the possibilities of an attack in your mind, and having the mindset necessary to use your gun to take a life to protect yours. If those things aren't already in place, don't carry your gun concealed. If you can't hit exactly what you aim at when the (range) conditions are calm, you probably won't hit what you aim at when all hell is breaking loose, outdoors, in low or no-light conditions, where bad guys tend to dwell.

Unless you've trained under induced-stress conditions (not just punching holes in paper targets on an easy Saturday at the range), your shooting arm will feel like a licorice stick and your eyes will narrow to a point where you won't even see your sights, much less be able to focus on the front one, and will be hard-pressed to line them both up accurately.

If you have to fight another male, even if he is smaller than you, who is jacked up on liquor, drugs, craziness, or more adrenaline than you, if you aren't ready, in bctter physical shape, and willing to do what it takes to win (and not just survive), you will be badly injured, disarmed, or killed.

If you cannot read the street signs and anticipate what might happen when one or more crooks comes near you, you will end up on the wrong end of victory, where the loss of your wallet and your pride will be a relief, compared to how bad it can really get.

If you aren't ready to think like a real crook, not some opportunistic jerk who is looking to make a quick score, but a hardcore, all-the-time bad guy, then you cannot protect your business, your belongings, and your most precious asset, the people who you love and care for.

This book is for those of you who have already seen the division of the world: sheep, wolves, and shepherds, and decided that you don't look good in wool.

Five things will save you (besides just your gun and enough ammo to reload it if necessary), your worldly goods, and your family or your business:

Live in the moment.

Most of the people go through life in Condition White, blissfully unaware of their safety, until something terrible happens. If they survive that bad experience, they quickly become hardened to their new world and they stop living in Condition White (unaware, missing the warning signs of danger, what just happened?). You can function in what firearms guru USMC Col. Jeff Cooper called "Condition Yellow" (aware, observant, and vigilant about your security) for the rest of your life. You can't live fulltime in Condition Red (fight back or escape) because it's simply too hard on your mind and body. (Most people can only operate in Condition Red for a few moments; if it goes on much longer than that, you're probably having a heart attack.)

Keep yourself in the position of maximum advantage.

Living in the "new normal," as some media types have labeled the post-9/11, post-Las Vegas massacre, post-school shootings era, now means that we must pay better attention to suspicious indicators. Simply put, in the streets, suspicious indicators are people, cars, situations, sights, and things that don't look, feel, sound, or smell right. The power of street-level intuition will be a constant theme in this book about using your Concealed Carry to your maximum advantage.

In his bestselling 1997 book ***The Gift of Fear***, security expert Gavin de Becker describes fear as "intuition's messenger." It literally tells you what to do, and if you're smart, you do it. He writes of a man who walked into a convenience store, felt very strong signals that something terrible was going to happen and left. Minutes later, a police officer walked in, interrupted a robbery in the store, was shot and killed. The man had seen many things that seemed "wrong" to him, that apparently, the officer did not.

Survival signals were given to us back when we all lived in caves and feared the darkness and the sounds roaring and snapping outside our homes. Intuitive feelings exist for a reason, and yet, how many people ignore them, rationalize them away, or worse yet, rationalize the irrational behavior of others. Consider the start of these street scenarios that will end badly for the unaware, the too–kind, or the less-than-vigilant: "That homeless guy looks like he needs some help" or "That woman asking me for money at the gas station is not a threat."

The position of maximum advantage says you choose a "tactical seat" at the fast-food restaurant (facing the door, in the corner, near an exit). It says you keep your car doors locked near transients who beg with cardboard signs at intersections. It says you make sure your child knows not to answer the front door without your permission. (And you don't just ask them to do it; you ***test*** them on it from time to time.)

Never, ever take the idea of security for granted.

In other words, stop complaining about what has been designed or installed to help you stay safe. As an example, when we use the remotes on our car key rings to deactivate the alarm and open the doors, we have to hit the button twice to unlock the passenger doors. And yet, when we only hit the door button once and go to open the back door and it's locked, at first we're peeved and we silently and wrongly curse the designers for building in this feature. But after hitting the button again, we thank them for their wisdom. Security was meant to be used and used correctly.

Never trade security for convenience.

As security consultants, when we have to show our IDs as we sign the visitor's log at a client's office building, before we complain inwardly about the hassle factor, we stop to appreciate the gesture.

When we're stripping off our shoes and belts for the trip through the metal detector at the airport (otherwise known as "bin Laden's revenge"), we're usually crabby about the intrusion, then we stop to think that part of living in the "new normal" means we are all treated to these inconveniences and eccentric accommodations, in the hopes that it will work when it is supposed to, as it is supposed to, and another shoe bomber doesn't get on a flight.

Through all this, we always have to remind ourselves: Don't make excuses; just do what you have to do. Yes, it's a hassle to take your keys out of the ignition when you're putting some mail in the mailbox next to the bus stop where a few people are sitting, but that's what keeps one of them from driving off with your car. Yes, it's faster to send your young daughter on a scavenger hunt at the grocery store, getting a few items while you shop, but you don't because it's not safe to leave her alone, even in that highly public environment.

In order to fight the enemy, we have to think like the enemy. This book encourages readers to protect themselves, their families, their assets, and their businesses, by seeing the world through the eyes of a good person surrounded by bad people. It teaches you to read the *real* street signs, not just the ones that say "STOP" or "Walk." Cops live longest when they can see what is not there. People are safest when they use their intuition and take assertive, aggressive action in the face of looming danger.

Crime and criminal behavior are complex matters. While there are no predictors of criminal violence, it is possible to study the patterns and motives of street criminals and reach a conclusion: *The best indicator of future criminal behavior is past criminal behavior.* In other words, criminals will seek out weaknesses in stores, facilities, cars, businesses, and with people, to victimize them, because those targets, and their approaches to take them down, has worked for them before.

While there are never any absolute methods or security devices to completely guarantee safety from criminal violence, my experience in law enforcement and criminology suggests that most "unprofessional" street criminals are lazy and spontaneously attracted to crimes of opportunity (e.g., they tend to choose unplanned, disorganized crimes over those requiring planning and/or premeditation). Their street behavior is often "episodically criminal" and highly emotional (e.g., they function "affectively," driven by fear and anger, as opposed to the more calm, predatory, unemotional, and organized professional criminals – a rarity these days).

These episodic street criminals are very often deterred by even the smallest, easiest, or most inexpensive security devices. Examples include: locked doors and secured windows on facilities and vehicles; security guards; car alarms, GPS locators, and engine kill switches; store or home signage describing alarms, cameras, or devices; strong lighting; the presence of witnesses; blocked access to the target (i.e., a cashier or a cab driver behind a security screen); blocked escape routes; and the vigilance and confidence of citizens who refused to act complacent, naïve, or afraid, so that they wouldn't be victimized. In other words, those who deterred a crook, fought fire with fire, hitting first, moving out fastest, and using their firearms accurately, legally, and effectively.

This book seeks to help Concealed Carry citizens who are fed up with feeling afraid, uneasy walking or working in their communities (often without really knowing why) to arm themselves properly, and to carry the tools, the weapons, and physical and psychological techniques they need to take back their lives.

This book is about changing, updating, and improving your Concealed Carry habits and giving you the tools of a warrior, so that you think like a shepherd and not act like a sheep. There will always be wolves; it's time to take up the staff of the shepherd and defend what is yours.

CHAPTER 1

MIKE'S EVERYDAY APPROACH TO CARRYING CONCEALED

After decades of taking on tasks where preparing and standing in harm's way was a chosen path, it's a given that I needed to be vigilant in order to protect my family and myself against evil people. My over-exposure to what goes bang in the dark drove me, like others, to take self-protection and being prepared to a higher state of awareness and readiness. Carrying Concealed can be defined as "the arming of yourself to act decisively when awareness and avoidance fails."

Of the many roles and responsibilities of instilling a protection mindset for myself and others, is having a "Concealed Carry System," a term that more accurately describes the Concealed Carry approach as having strong situational awareness, avoiding dangerous situations when possible, and when all else fails, maintaining a scenario-based "what to do if" skill set in order to act in a timely way to defend yourself and others.

An important note to consider as you read our book is that this collection of instruction, comments, and approaches are based upon our years of training, experience, and adjustments to the new and morphing threats we all face. There isn't one way or one fix to defending yourself. What we have realized is the necessity of a strong commitment to increasing our awareness to avoid threatening situations or to act with practiced efficiency, as critical keys to being responsible Concealed Carriers.

Like we have, you'll need to create a balanced approached to Carrying Concealed. This will require finding the right weapon, understanding scenario-based situations that include "what if," responses, and having a regular Concealed Carry training regimen.

We all know people who have weapons they do not regularly fire, carry, or even clean. So let this book help further your understanding and preparation for Carrying Concealed.

Our Concealed Carry System is broken down into Knowledge Zones. These include: knowing yourself, knowing your gear, having awareness, being in avoidance mode, and knowing when to take action. Knowing your core abilities, your stress reactions to fear or surprise events, and having decent general physical fitness is essential to carrying a concealed weapon. You must develop these interconnected skills in order to remain aware, to see developing safety and security concerns or immediate threats, and to be ready to initiate avoidance techniques.

And your ability to act versus react to threatening events can only be developed and practiced through range training and stress testing. Your every day carry (EDC) gear should include one or, preferably, two handguns; an edged weapon you know how to use; a mini flashlight; spare magazines; and emergency means to stop bleeding, meaning a combat tourniquet.

You also want to avoid printing (the outline of your weapon showing through your clothing) and must have practiced the means to quickly draw and use your Concealed Carry tools if warranted. In order to have a properly-purposed weapon for your Concealed Carry System, you must know your type of weapon, your type of round, the total number of rounds at your disposal, your type of holster (including its strengths, weaknesses, and limitations), your mental awareness, and the mindset to get ahead of a directed threat.

One consideration of your Concealed Carry approach is deciding what to wear. It depends on where you're going, what the weather is like, and whether you'll be mostly driving, sitting, or standing. Current Concealed Carry rules vary from state to state, with an assortment of additional rules and exceptions strewn throughout the varying regulations, which can create some rather interesting challenges. If you have decided to Carry Concealed, obtained your permit, continued with your training, and accepted the responsibility, then you must ensure that you are following and managing the challenges presented by carrying a gun. We will not go into great depth matching your specific role with every set rule, but rather, we will share considerations that could assist your preparedness in Carrying Concealed.

Living the Concealed Carry lifestyle has us considering each phase of our day and preparing for that period with the means to protect ourselves and others. At home, in and around the truck/car, at work, and out and about, there is a

prepared and properly-purposed means to use a firearm if necessary. Preparedness includes practiced rules of engagement. There are very few situations you may encounter that should surprise you. Consider your environment, what activity is around you, and what potentially good or maybe bad people are around you?

For example, you decide to go shopping at the local market and pull into the parking lot. What can happen here? Carjacking, strong-arm robbery, armed robbery, purse snatching, confronted by begging homeless guy, car accident, a fight between others, an accident, a medical event? Just because you have a gun, which of these should you or would you get involved with, if any?

In this scenario, the environment is the parking lot. Parking lots can be the location of crimes against people and property. There is a chance of an incident in the lot, so the environment presents a risk. Next, we look at the people in the lot. There could be a bad actor with nefarious intent to steal or harm someone. Who could it be? There are always possible victims or targets for the bad actor. It could be the lady sitting in her car with the door open while texting or talking on her phone. It could be the elderly lady loading groceries into her trunk, with her purse still in the shopping cart. Or it could be the two teenagers, seemingly lost in the fun of their new relationship.

By analyzing the environment and recognizing the scenarios that could occur, in terms of potential threat, you are actually getting ahead of the threat curve by reading the scene to ultimately avoid an issue.

The three big A's in self-protection are: Awareness, Avoidance, and Action. Being Aware of the possible threats and looking for related concerning behaviors can allow you to avoid situations. This could mean leaving the area, or if a life-threatening situation presents itself, pulling your concealed firearm for your ultimate survival.

Your everyday approach to Carrying Concealed requires a self-examination of what you do, where you go, and what you will decide to do in order to protect yourself. Matching your schedule with your preparation is an important key to your successful Concealed Carry lifestyle.

Consider another scenario: Leaving your safe and secure home, you drive to the gym early one morning for a quick workout. Are you wearing your gym clothes or carrying them in? The sun is still not up as you park in the lot of your local fitness center and walk in. Is your gun on you, in your gym bag, or did you leave it in your car? You leave the gym, and driving with your seatbelt on, head to your favorite morning coffee stop. You walk in to order your special double-tap latte. Seeing the morning regulars, you get your coffee and sit down to catch up on the local gossip. Where is your gun now? Each of these situations presents a challenge to carrying and gaining access to your firearm.

We all have our routines and daily challenges: dropping the kids off at school, heading in and out of office buildings, stores, and restaurants. Our everyday approach to Carrying Concealed requires thought, preparation and readiness. Carrying Concealed is much more than filling out a form, taking a class, and buy a revolver or a semi-automatic pistol. Our everyday approach requires us to consider many factors and it will take time to develop a normal, routine ability to safely carry and maintain an always vigilant posture.

This book, along with additional training, and self-reflection of your daily schedule and your purpose for Carrying Concealed, will create the proper mindset for self-protection and survival. Surprises are not your friend. It's usually the direct result of a stimulating situation that we have not mentally prepared ourselves for. Our bodies take over during a life-threatening surprise. Only through practice and the mental preparation of pre-event planning for any possible threat scenarios we can avoid freezing, panicking, or responding in a way that could cause greater harm to ourselves or others.

CHAPTER 2

GETTING CCW INSURANCE

You should start by expecting to get sued by anyone you point a gun at, shoot at, hit and wound, or hit and kill. Either the perpetrator will sue you or his aggrieved family will sue you, because prior to threatening to rob, rape, or kill you or your family, this person was on his way to church, heading to a meeting with the Pope, or had the cure for cancer in his front pocket, and you snuffed at this person at the prime of his life or right when he was trying to get his act together (stay off drugs, report to his parole officer, help little old ladies across the street).

We're always amazed at the outrage the family members of the dead bad guy show to the press, admitting that their loved one (who they've often not seen for years, or been estranged from, or they had kicked out of their homes because they stole from them, used drugs in their presence, or otherwise threatened them) was such a "giving, loving person."

The "grieving family" in these cases probably hated the dead guy and may be secretly glad that he's gone. They always say they want "justice," which really means they'd prefer "money" and most of it coming from you.

Because of the likelihood of being sued, you need CCW insurance, which provides you with fees to pay a criminal defense lawyer and monies to defend yourself and protect your way of life. Although this is a niche insurance product, kind of like insurance your valuable coin collection or a piece of art, it's more common than ever now. There are several ways you can cover yourself:

The Concealed Carry Association of America (usconcealedcarry.com) offers membership, a great magazine (that Steve writes for occasionally), and insurance policies at various levels.

The National Rifle Association (www.nra.org) offers membership in a gun rights organization that has been around since 1871, and insurance policies through its NRA Carry Guard policies with Lockton Affinity.

You can ask you're the broker who writes your homeowner's insurance for either an umbrella or a jumbo policy that may be able to cover you for the lawful use of your firearm.

Some of these policies will not only cover your criminal defense attorney's fees, but bail money as well, both of which can be substantial in shooting cases with injuries or deaths.

Speak to your broker about the necessary adding coverage or, look for specific coverage from insurance brokers or firms that provide this type of rare but necessary coverage.

Insurance people are in the business of writing and selling policies, in all kinds of creative and innovative ways. Talk to them and ask them what they can do or who they can refer you to.

The popularity of so-called "pre-paid legal" programs, where you pay a monthly fee that serves as a retainer for an attorney. (Legal Shield is the most popular type of these programs.) With these plans, you can use an attorney for a business dispute or a landlord-tenant conflict, and for criminal defense. Check and see if you can just buy a criminal defense package.

Since Steve lives (armed) in Colorado and travels (armed) to California for work a few times per month, he has two criminal defense lawyers on retainer in Colorado and one in California, all ready to help him that he needs a defense. (Their fees would be paid for by his Platinum membership with USCCA.)

If we go back to the US Navy SEAL motto that "two is one and one is none," and the same is just as true with people as well as devices, then you'll want to develop a business connection with at least two criminal defense attorneys. Once you identify and contact the criminal defense lawyers you want to use from your community, it makes sense to meet in person or over the phone with those professionals and say some version of, "I'm a responsible CCW permit holder in this state. I have no intention of using my gun in a reckless way, only to lawfully protect myself or my family should the need ever arise. Can I give you a copy of my permit and all my contact information, including my insurance policy, which includes criminal defense fees? Can I get your after-hours contact information?" You may have to or want to pay these lawyers a small retainer, just to have them start a file for you, but this is not always a requirement.

Once you have that relationship in place, spend a few minutes at least once per year, re-contacting those two attorneys by phone or email and re-introduce yourself. It's useful, we believe, to rekindle these relationships each year, provide updated contact information for yourself and your family, and make certain the attorneys can still serve your needs.

Keep your policy information and attorney contacts in your wallet, car, and range bag.

Having one to two criminal defense lawyers on standby to keep you out of jail, and having the necessary insurance policy or policies with the funds to pay for the (whopping high) legal fees and protect your assets is just part of the cost of doing business these days, especially as a CCW permit holder. Write the check and go about the business of your life knowing that you have the protection you may never need or you may have to use tomorrow.

CHAPTER 3

MIKE'S MUST-HAVE GEAR LIST AND WHY

One of the most uncomfortable feelings I have encountered over the years is that nagging concern: "What have I forgotten to bring with me to keep myself and my family safe?" To help ward off that feeling, I've adopted checklists, read gear reviews, and practiced double-checks. But, as luck would have it, many trips and events I've been involved with have reinforced the concept that living by a checklist alone may actually create a situation of less preparedness. Over-reliance on checklists flattens our thinking and inhibits our ability to assess, analyze, and determine best-case solutions.

To avoid forgetting something, I create lists. On a trip, the list may include things like: enough clothing for five days, a toiletry kit, dental floss, and vitamins. My Concealed Carry gear list might include: my gun, two spare magazines, my magazine and weapon holster or carrying devices, my flashlight, a tactical tourniquet, my gun belt, my Concealed Carry permit, my insurance card, my phone, my knife, and a pen. These lists may appear complete at first glance and many might say that this is obviously all that is necessary for a trip. Some others might just say, "I don't need a list to remember."

As the years have gone by, I have found that the lists were not enough, or were not thorough enough to address the varying situations my trips included. Could a list be sufficient for going to the market, or the bank, or out for a walk? Maybe. It depends. My daily list may say: go to the bank, go to the market, and walk the dog. The question is, does the list cover the gear I need to safely carry my gun or associated gear to the bank, to the market, and for a walk with the dog? Of course, it doesn't. Most standard Concealed Carry gear lists recommend the following: gun, magazine, mindset, and holsters. Should your daily activity list have a gear list aligned with that day's activity? Yes, it should.

I have found that many lists are incomplete and don't match the purpose I may be carrying a gun for. Additionally, lists are more like guidelines for planning and require deeper consideration of a number of things before we can say we have a complete gear list. We have ultimately determined that lists are useful, but for the Concealed Carry lifestyle, a stronger approach necessitates consideration of the essential gear linked to a potential situation or the purpose of our activity.

There is no doubt that some will call this over-preparedness or being overly-cautious but let me ask you this: Has anyone involved in a shooting situation ever run out of bullets? Has anyone in a stressful situation had a flashlight battery die? Has someone carrying a gun involved in a shooting situation been injured and needed a tourniquet? What about someone Carrying Concealed who did not have his or her permit when asked by a law enforcement officer? And do you know who you are going to call to assist you (besides just 9-1-1) if people are injured to killed in a shooting?

The most important tool in your tool box rests upon your shoulders: your mind and your ability to reason out various situations. Every carry situation begins and ends with your mind. We always approach the Concealed Carry lifestyle as a system that includes Awareness, Avoidance, and, when needed, decisive Action. Our mind drives us through our study, preparedness, and practice, and the ability to create Awareness of the places we visit. Awareness is our ability to understand the operational space we might be in and how the safety and security concerns of that space can be threatening to us.

Being Aware allows us to detect and determine potential threatening situations that we could Avoid. Avoidance of an incident is the safer course of action and avoids the negative potential outcomes if action is taken. Action is when all else fails and the ultimate survival of self or others requires the use of your ready gear. After a violent incident or shooting, it's the preparation of such an outcome where you know what to do and whom to call to ensure the potentially tragic event ends in the best possible way for you, the Concealed Carrier. This is why we say your tool box begins and ends with your mindset and your preparation. Therefore, our must-have approach to our gear requires a deeper understanding of our mindset, our carry situations, and on-going evaluation of proper gear purposed to your use needs.

Carry situations depend upon many factors. We'll stipulate that the need to carry is a given right and a core belief in protecting yourself and your family. Other factors include where the situation occurs, when and how it occurs, what occurs. The situation might occur in a home, on a ranch, in a motorhome touring the US, on daily errands, or during business or work. Surprisingly, many people who Carry Concealed carry their weapons inconsistently and without a plan. It's suggested in many gun articles and on gun websites, and we agree, that if you're legally permitted to carry, you should always carry.

There is no reason to believe that you only need to carry in the evening, to and from your favorite restaurant, or that you should leave your gun in your car while at the gym, or running in the convenience store to get a cup of coffee If you are permitted to carry, you should always carry, as we cannot know when and where we will need to enact our survival system.

The gear list question, as tied to a pending situation is: What gun or type of gear do I need, and how can I carry it all depending upon the activity I am choosing? During summer, out at the lake or jet skiing is a different situation than in the mountains, walking along a frozen lake trail. We'll discuss round selection in a later chapter; it's an important consideration when determining the best bullet type for self-defense.

A summer carry can be different than a winter carry. A carry situation while the carrier is seated and seat-belted in a car is different than the carry situation when the carrier is driving a motorcycle. To help address carry gear, we must therefore plan ahead to align our gear selections with those situations, places, and activities where we plan to carry.

Carry gear situations are varying, but some common use cases are worth sharing. Each reader can adjust his or her individual lifestyle and carry situations to build upon the following core examples. My core carry gear list includes the following: mindset, (multiple) knives, flashlights, holsters, spare magazines, first-aid kits (every day carry EDC and full kits), CCW permits (two copies for each State), my conceal carry legal assistance and insurance cards, weapon-mounted light with laser, and my survival attitude.

Home carry situations allow me to have the most gear dispersed to each properly purposed area in my house. Home invasions are a concern for most, and none of us are immune to the possibilities. Practicing our Three A's, starting with Awareness, my desire is to get ahead of a potential threat by evaluating the risks to my property and to prepare my gear and means to protect my home and family.

Most break-ins are actually "walk-ins," in which homes could have been more secure if the residents had simply used their locks on doors and windows. Once I evaluate my property and create security measures to avoid having it look like a prime target for a nefarious actor, I can stage my gear. This will include several guns, knives, and flashlights (and spare batteries) dispersed around my home. Gear should have a dedicated spot and a purpose for its location that is still rendered safe for visitors, kids, and the elderly. Homes with safe rooms require an extra full set of gear, spare batteries, and survival essentials. Members of the house should all know where each gear item is, as well as their use and purpose. Families should have training sessions together to develop code words or phrases as alerts. Additionally, willing family members could train for low-light and room-clearing situations or safe dry-firing or laser target drills.

Vehicle gear lists, like those for the home, enable the

Concealed Carrier to have a full set of gear at his or her disposal. However, there is a greater challenge to keeping your vehicle secure and to prevent it from falling into a bad guy's control. For my vehicles, my gear list includes: mindset, guns, spare magazines, two types of carry holsters, flashlights, knives, first-aid kit, CCW permits, legal aid and insurance card, tow service card, secured/attached weapon lock boxes, an alarm, and an alarm sticker.

The key to carrying in vehicles is having the means to grab, un-holster, and use your gun, if needed, as well as being able to secure your gear. What this means is that if you are carrying appendix, Outside the Waistband (OWB), and you're not able to get to your gun, then you need to have either an ankle rig or a holster that allows for quick and safe draw without crossing (pointing a loaded weapon across your own body or that of another person, potentially hurting someone if it discharges.) Also for vehicle carries, a person needs to have the means to reach his or her first-aid kit or window breaching tools while strapped in the driver's seat.

My "out and about" gear includes: guns, knives, flashlights, my EDC first-aid kit, my permits, legal aid and insurance card, and a backpack or everyday carry bag. It is in our "out and about" times that we find folks just grabbing their weapons, shoving them into their waistbands, and doing what they do, feeling safe with just their guns. In discussing their carry preparation, they'll agree that they should have more, but then fall back on the statement, "I've always carried like this, and nothing has ever happened."

Herein lies the decision to either do what's right as a standard, or to just get by based upon the thought that nothing is likely to happen. "Okay," they say, "I have survived to this point by just shoving my gun in my pocket or waistband and nothing has happened. I'm also the person who found himself in a low-light situation without a flashlight, or with a flashlight with dead batteries. I'm also the person who needed a knife and didn't have it."

I recently read about a kid playing on a playground who snagged his hood. Surrounded by parents and others who didn't have a means to cut the hood tie, they watched in horror as the child hung helplessly. There was the case of a man who got his tie snagged in an escalator belt and was choked to death. I will always have a knife with me. Nothing may happen, but the consequence of being unprepared is unacceptable to me. The weighing of "security versus convenience" is a constant struggle and an individual choice, but doing it right every time is a goal we should accept and with that acceptance, we also embrace the extra challenge to always be prepared.

So why does it matter to be properly prepared and purposed? I believe we each have a core duty to protect ourselves and our families, without having to count on others. Our gear list to Carry Concealed begins and ends with our ability to think, reason, and practice Awareness, Avoidance, and practiced Actions.

Your considerations should include: What happens if I'm involved in an incident? If and when a situation happens there will be a deep look by many outsiders at the environment and the people involved in the situation. Could it have been avoided, using every possible means? If, in the review of the incident, it's shown that you, as the Concealed Carrying citizen practiced strong Awareness, Avoidance, Action thinking, and preparation, the outcome should indicate every step you followed to avoid the incident until you had to act to protect yourself. The time it takes to plan, prepare, and maintain the proper gear is much less of an expense than the physical and emotional costs of not being prepared.

If we carry a gun we must consider that there exists a chance of being shot or injured by a gun, meaning yours or someone else's. From training to situational incidents, injuries happen, and being unprepared and under-equipped can be deadly if we don't have the means to self-administer first-aid.

EDC includes having the means to stop bleeding, cover sucking chest wounds, and hang on until emergency medical services arrive. All too frequently, police receive reports of AD's (accidental discharges) which in reality are NDs (negligent discharges) at the range, training sites, in homes, and in cars. During poorly-supervised gun training, a gun holder may accidentally shoot himself or herself in the leg or foot while practicing draws or re-holstering. Cleaning a loaded gun (who does this?) or not properly clearing a weapon before storing it has led to accidental shootings at homes and workplaces.

What happens just after a shooting occurs is time-critical in saving your own or other's lives. Having EDC first-aid kits are keys to our survival. Our EDC kits have two tourniquets, a dual sucking chest wound patch, gloves, and pressure bandages. Every Concealed Carry permit holder should have training in basic first-aid for shooting wounds to self-survive or to provide aid to others.

Gear lists are not just checklists, but rather guidelines to ensure we look at our daily situations and use strong Awareness, Avoidance, and Action thinking aligned with our necessary gear.

Basic Gear List:

Mindset
Understanding of the Three A's
Conceal Carry Permit
Insurance
Guns
Spare magazines
Holsters fit for varying carry situations
Flashlights
Knives
EDC first aid kit

CHAPTER 4

LEARN TO STOP THE BLEEDING, LITERALLY

If you carry a gun, know this: Tourniquets save lives and you should know how to use one. It's called "Rescuing Yourself" or saving the life of another, maybe even including the bad guy you just shot. (Which looks a lot better to a judge, jury, or prosecutor then standing there and just watching him bleed out.)

Another shooting at a high school or college campus. Another church shooting. Another shooting at a mall or a movie theater. The list of these events gets longer and sadly, more frequent. If there is a bad guy with a gun where you or others are at, and you or they are injured with a wound that could bleed out, the response time by the paramedics could be long enough to be fatal. The police will arrive on scene to stop the shooter, not provide immediate first-aid to you. The EMTs may not go inside the facility until it is safe for them to do so. Therefore, you must become the saver of your life and the lives of others who get wounded. That's the bad news. The good news is you can do that, if you get trained on how to use a tourniquet and/or to pack a bleeding wound.

And if you don't think you'll ever be at a place where someone starts shooting with a gun, okay. But consider the myriad of ways you, or someone you care about, or a complete stranger, could be injured badly enough to bleed out. This includes car accidents, home accidents, shootings or suicide attempts, or accidents in public places that are serious enough to cause an open wound, an avulsion, or a full or partial amputation. You can buy a combat-level tourniquet, on Amazon, as one example, for about $20. It's small enough to fit into your purse, backpack, or glove compartment. Consider this: Uncontrolled bleeding is the number one cause of preventable death from trauma.

After the Sandy Hook school shooting in 2012, an emergency medicine protocol called the Hartford Consensus (https://www.facs.org/about-acs/hartford-consensus) was created by trauma surgeons and other concerned medical and law enforcement professionals to train law enforcement and the public to be able to address life-threatening shooting injuries following mass casualty events, without always having to wait for paramedics to come inside. The life you save may be a stranger's, a family member's, or even your own, since you can apply a tourniquet or direct pressure to your own wound and live to tell about it.

Although emergency healthcare is certainly stressful and complex, and many patients have multiple issues that can threaten their lives, the solutions to preventing them from bleeding to death are two: use a tourniquet placed just above a bleeding limb and/or pack or stuff the open wound with bandages (or even a t-shirt or the victim's socks) and use direct, continuous pressure on the area until medical help arrives.

According to www.BleedingControl.org, who offer one-hour free "Stop the Bleed" training classes, here are the necessary steps to stop someone from bleeding to death:

Ensure your own safety. You can't take care of someone if the scene is not safe, and you're not safe from immediate harm. In other words, the lifeguards can't drown at the beach, so your first order of care is to yourself. If you have to move the victim to provide care, then do it. Wear gloves anytime you're near blood-borne pathogens.

A - Alert someone to call 9-1-1 and report back to you that he or she did.

B – Bleeding site: Where is it? Cut, tear, or remove the victim's clothing to find it specifically (be wearing gloves that this point). Could be more than one bleeding site. Look for blood that spurts or pulses, (which suggests an arterial bleed), pools, soaks the victim's clothing or existing bandages, or is coming from the full or partial loss of a limb. Serious bleeding can make people confused, agitated, or even combative, until they lapse into unconsciousness.

C – Compress the bleeding wound, by applying direct pressure, pack as much gauze for other material into the wound, and cover the area with a clean cloth (anything you can find to use from the patient's or your body or a first-aid kit). Push on the wound site with both hands (one on top of the other, like you would position your hands when doing CPR). Or use a tourniquet, placed two or three inches above the wound site and tightened down (and never loosened) until the bleeding stops. The goal is simple, even in the stress of that moment: compress bleeding blood vessels to stop the flow. Keep the pressure on by hand until relieved by paramedics. Doctors are the only ones who should remove a tourniquet.

The old thinking about tourniquets has changed, thanks largely to their frequent use in combat theaters in Iraq and Afghanistan. Tourniquets can be in place for up to two hours without causing permanent damage to the patient's limb. They aren't useful for wounds in the shoulder, neck (and never around a victim's throat), or groin; that will require wound packing and a fast run to a hospital by the paramedics. They should never be placed around a joint, like a knee, wrist, elbow, hip or shoulder; using them there damages the joint and does not stop the blood flow sufficiently enough.

And the previous Boy Scouts thinking about using belts, cloths, ropes, or other similar ligatures as tourniquets is no longer appropriate. These attempts can cause more damage to the wound and surrounding nerves, so it's best to use a combat-type tourniquet that features a wide nylon band and a t-shaped device called a "windlass" that can be tightened and clamped into place. Paramedics and doctors want anyone who applies a tourniquet to themselves or to an injured person to write the time the device was applied, either on the patient's forehead (e.g., T-1035, for tourniquet applied at 1035 hours) or on the tourniquet itself if there is a space.

Tourniquets hurt quite a lot when they are applied correctly, because they impinge nerves and blood vessels. That means they are working properly. Despite a patient's long and pitiful complaints, they should never be loosened to check for bleeding or to help the victim feel better. Paramedics can give people pain medications for their discomfort, but the purpose of the tourniquet is to go on and stay on.

Your local hospital may offer a free training program called

"Stop the Bleed," that covers in more detail what you've read here, and give you the chance to practice using tourniquets and stopping blood flow on mannequin limbs. You can take the short course yourself or schedule at your workplace with your colleagues. Go to www.BleedingControl.org for more information. Like knowing how to give CPR or operate an AED device, stopping someone from bleeding to death is a skill that takes some training, practice, and forethought. You can do this!

CHAPTER 5

COMBAT APPLICATION TOURNIQUET (CAT) USE AND FIRST-AID BAG ESSENTIALS

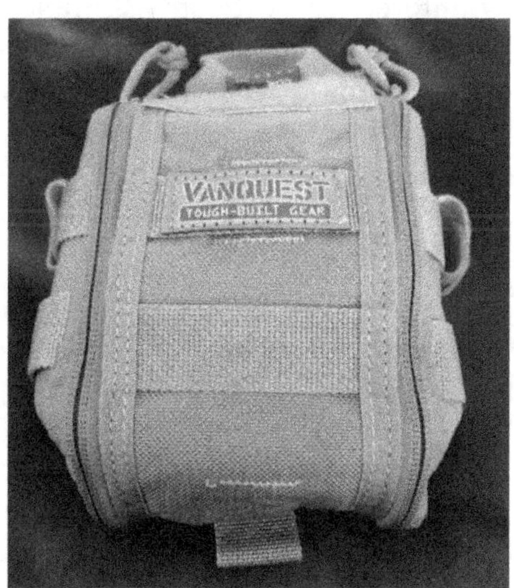

Range Bag by Tim Smith of Provisional Survival Concepts

It is imperative that we continue to learn from past incidents in order to prepare us for future events. The lifestyle of Carrying Concealed is the acceptance that we are willing to stand in harm's way to protect ourselves and others. In our preparation, we study the hard lessons of self-defense situations, targeted violence events, mass shootings, and methods-to-survive incidents where Awareness, Avoidance, and Action may have failed.

After the Sandy Hook school massacre, an effort called "Stop the Bleed" was created by concerned medical and law enforcement responders in Hartford, CT to address mass casualty events. The issue which created the urgency for "Stop the Bleed" centered on the dynamic challenge of targeted mass shooting events, law enforcement active shooter responses, and the need to save multiple casualties at the scene, instead of at a hospital. The first challenge for law enforcement in arriving at active shooter events is to stop the attacker. It's the goal of the paramedics to save as many lives as possible once the threat is over. In their responses, law enforcement officers assemble, make entry, and move toward the sound of gunfire, passing possibly injured, seriously bleeding, and helpless victims. To end the threat, law enforcement must move quickly, with determination to save lives from the bad guy. It's not their primary role to provide first-aid, except to other wounded cops which is always their mandate.

However, blood loss is the reported leading cause of preventable death associated with targeted violence such as active shootings because of the delays in getting the paramedics to the victims. A victim of a shooting, at an incident, home, or at the range could die in minutes if the wound is left unattended. The "Stop the Bleed" campaign was created to train and empower the public involved in accidents, serious injury events, or active shooter incidents to initiate lifesaving techniques to stop the number one cause of death — blood loss. As we just said in the previous chapter, knowing your ABC's applies here: Alert

– Bleeding – Compression.

Alert

This relates to our on-going discussions about Awareness and Avoidance. Be alert to the situation, avoid complicating the situation, or causing harm to yourself. Remain behind cover or remove yourself or others, including injured people, from an unsafe position to a safer one.

Bleeding

Find the source of bleeding. This could be difficult and without obvious pools of blood, we may not know where the source of the injury could be. This in itself can contribute to the patient's loss of life, so it's imperative to search thoroughly for wounds. Finding the bleeding source when it's not obvious may require opening, cutting off, or removing clothing. For chest injuries, it's essential to look for both the entry and exit wounds. A common error is finding a chest wound and putting a chest seal on the front of the victim's torso, but not finding the exit wound which continues to cause blood loss.

Compression

Apply pressure to stop the bleeding at the source. Compression might be applied directly on the wound by packing it with gauze or cloth, or for wounds to arms or legs, using a tourniquet.

The ability to save lives through bleeding control has been reinforced by other mass casualty events such as the Boston Marathon bombing and Las Vegas concert mass shooting.

Each of these events, although horrible for the loss of life, reinforced how the control of bleeding can save additional lives.

Our AAA Model - "Awareness, Avoidance, and Action" - requires pre-planning, preparation, and practice. For the Action phase, when all else has failed, it's important to be prepared. Actions to survive your own injuries may include self-controlling your severe bleeding with your own tourniquet.

If you are involved in a self-defense shooting incident or a range training incident, having the right first-aid gear, a survival frame of mind, and the ability to self-administer, is critical to saving your life or others' lives.

We have multiple medical carry kits that complement our readiness. These include our range bags, which we take when training at any range and a car kit for driving across country or out and about. We have secondary Combat Application Tourniquets (CATs) in each bag. Every person who reads this, carries a gun, and goes out in public, should know the basics to "Stop the Bleed." Everyone should have at least basic first-aid training and each of us should frequently practice caring for wounds and injuries we may face. This is part of being prepared.

The tourniquet can be lifesaving, is easy to carry, and when used correctly, is an easy-to-use device to control and stop major bleeding. Let's look at how and why they work:

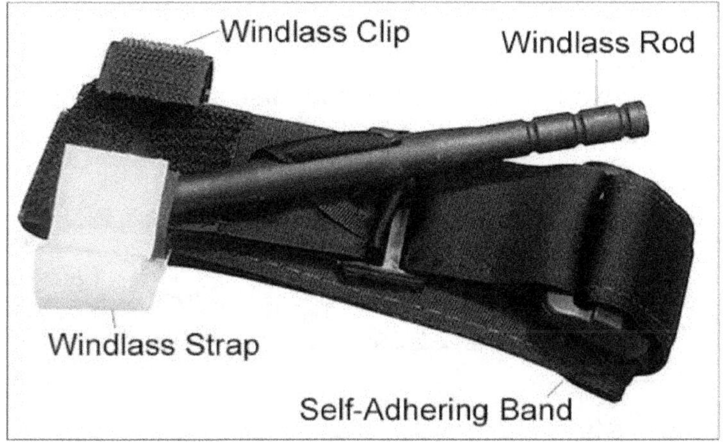

Photo courtesy of Composite Resources, Inc.

The CAT is the preferred tourniquet for field use that allows the user to either self-administer or apply it to others. It's easy to store and to pack in your daily EDC gear, so the invaluable tourniquet is a must-have tool.

Everyone should take first-aid or Stop the Bleed-type training to reinforce their CAT use. The basics are: find the wound, place the CAT two to three inches above the wound (not over joints or around the neck), secure it (remove the slack), tighten the Windlass Rod down until the bleeding stops, and then secure the Windlass Rod with the Velcro Windlass Strap. It's a myth to follow the old recommendation to loosen the tourniquet every couple hours to check on or save the limb. Once the CAT is applied, only medical professionals should remove the tourniquet. (Use a pen to write on the victim's forehead the time the CAT was applied.)

Another reported fact is that tourniquets are not comfortable and will likely hurt when used properly. The important point in this technique is saving a person's life through the control of his or her bleeding. Be supportive

and talk with your victim, providing updates on what you are doing and why.
Injuries and wounds to the chest and torso are not served by a tourniquet. We keep "chest seals" in each range and first-aid kits.

Chest wounds or sucking chest wounds occur when a bullet penetrates the chest cavity. Air escaping the lungs can ultimately create pressure inside the chest cavity, collapsing one or both lungs, and putting pressure on the heart.

Emergency field treatment for chest wounds includes finding the wound (both entry and exit) and sealing it (on one or both sides of the victim's torso) to prevent air from escaping. The chest seals in our kits have adhesive patches for easy applications. The key for dealing with chest wounds is to be sure that you have checked the victim's front, back, and sides for additional wounds. A common error is to treat the first found wound and not look for additional injuries.

Body cavity wounds require compression dressings to both fill and stop the bleeding from the cavity. Compression bandages for wound care cover regular gauze and hemostatic dressings. Hemostatic dressings have blood clotting material to assist in the bleeding control process. Bleeding control impregnated hemostatic dressings are now part of tactical medical kits.

Treatment of these wounds starts with clearing the wound area of clothes, removing pooling blood, packing the wound with a hemostatic dressing, and then securing with compression dressings.

This chapter can in no way fully address the necessary training required to treat these types of wounds. What we hope to achieve is to bring to light the importance of having basic medical aid tools and training as part of the Concealed Carry preparation and lifestyle. If we carry a gun and are willing to stand in harm's way, we must know the basics to save a life, whether it's your own, a bystander to your shooting incident, and even for the person who tried to harm you.

CHAPTER 6

HOW NOT TO CREATE NEGLIGENT DISCHARGES

Let's start by getting our terminology absolutely, mechanically, and accurately correct. When a gun that you are holding fires in a way, in a direction, or in a place it's not supposed to, it's your fault. Stop using the phrase "accidental discharge," because it's just not true. It's not an accidental discharge – the gun didn't just "go off by itself" or it didn't just "fire when you were cleaning it." You or someone around you made a mistake with both the state of "unloadedness" and the trigger, and if you're able to read this now, that means you're still alive to tell the tale and you - or the other person who was (mis)handling your gun – didn't kill you or himself or herself.

The moves you make while holding or manipulating your gun or any gun are intentional, or they had better be. In some form or fashion, these reasons for a negligent discharge are always your fault. You either mishandled your gun, let someone else mishandle your gun, or you allowed your gun to get out of perfect working order. If it's loaded with functioning ammo and the trigger mechanism can activate the hammer or the striker toward that ammo, then it's always susceptible to a negligent discharge. This holds true for all of your revolvers, pistols, rifles, and shotguns. Even guns you think "don't work anymore" or "bad ammo" (wet, oily, rusty, corroded, bent, etc.) can still discharge.

We're not gunsmiths, so this is not a deep dive into all of the various things that can go wrong with firearms, since there are many. The point is to keep the barrel of anything pointed safely away from you or any other non-target, be careful with all ammo you handle, and keep your trigger finger completely away from all triggers.

While it may seem like an accident at the time, what follows are the various ways and means you can create a negligent discharge:

Stress – Your mind is on other things, you're not paying attention to your safety situation, and you lose focus on what's important: no muzzle sweeps, background knowledge, finger off the trigger, ammo awareness.

Showing off for a buddy or a loved one – Anytime you mix goofing around and/or alcohol, and/or showing off in front of someone, either at home or at the range, the chance for a negligent discharge exists. Keep your head in your game and stay mature when around your firearms. And don't let other people, whether you know them or not, mess around near you. This includes strangers at the range, who may be seconds away from a negligent discharge unless you tell the Rangemaster or intervene.

Hammer cocked back into single-action mode on your revolver – If you know revolvers, and you should, you know with the hammer cocked back into single-action mode (the hammer goes one way, forward, instead of backwards and forwards in double-action mode), not only is the movement of the firing pin to the primer of your round that much shorter, the trigger pull lessens dramatically. Since the trigger moves back so far, even the slightest contact will cause it to fire. It's possible your cocked revolver could fire if you drop it just right. More likely is your having your finger in the trigger guard and touching the trigger before you're on target and ready to actually fire the gun.

Broken gun or magazines – If you're not a professional gunsmith, you may not know your gun is broken until you go to use it. As an example, you won't know you have a broken firing pin until you get a series of soft strikes on your rounds. Therefore, treat your gun as it could fail at any moment because it just might. Machines break all the time, even when we do our best to keep them lubed and clean. As such, you can't completely trust your machines (gun and mags) not to fail at some point in owning them, or when you least expect it.

Bad, wet, rusted, corroded, dirty, old, or oily ammo – If you drop bad ammo on to a concrete floor, it may fire off. If you have old or unstable powder in your ammo, it can go off in odd and unexpected ways, like when it's exposed to intense heat. Check your mags and your ammo and don't be a cheapskate; get rid of bad bullets.

Low light or darkness – While you should know how to load, reload, unload, and operate your gun in low light conditions, darkness is not your fired when it comes to being safe. Don't assume that what you saw in daylight is still the same in low light and no light.

Not developing your muscle memory – You need to keep repeating and refining your dry fire, range training, and Concealed Carry safety habits to build those neural pathways for success. Having built-in safety routines will keep you from doing something stupid or fatal because you had a brain freeze. As an example, we always check our weapons for readiness every day, before we leave the house in Concealed Carry mode, even though no one has touched them since the night before.

Not being familiar with the pistol when carrying a 1911-type pistol in the ready position – There are a lot of stories of negligent discharges when carrying a 1911-style pistol with a round in the chamber and the hammer back. And, there are lots of Concealed Carriers who carry that way with never a problem or a negligent discharge. Know your gun, know your ammo, know your holster and carrying style, and know your limitations.

Bad holster or careless carrying habits – Plenty of stories exist where people have shot themselves in their groin, legs, or feet because they grabbed an unholstered gun with the wrong grip, usually in a hurry to pull it. Guns always need holsters and effective holsters have trigger covers. Use the proper holster for the gun type, e.g., pocket guns need pocket holsters. Don't mix and match your holsters unless you're positive they will fit each gun snugly and safely. Better to have a tight gun than one that falls out if you bend, run, or move quickly.

Taking someone's word that the gun is unloaded, the ammo is old, or it's all inoperable – The phrase, "That gun or that ammo hasn't worked in 50 years" is often followed by a surprising and loud band just after it is said.

Military EOD teams still get called to disarm and dismantle live hand grenades and live unexploded bombs from WWI. Treat old stuff as if it will still work.

Not knowing your gun or the gun you're firing – You should know your own gun and how it fires your ammo. Period. Always perform safety checks on guns and ammo loaned to you by your friends. Do visual inspections and handle them as if they were your own, loaded and ready to fire.

Not being methodical in your movements – When you're in a hurry or moving too fast you can skip safety steps. Slow it down on the range when you're preparing to fire for the first time or when you are getting ready to clean your gun at home. Follow the safety steps at the range to the letter. Make sure your ammo is in another room for any dry fire or gun cleaning activities.

Tired, sleepy, or not concentrating – It's easy to make stupid mistakes with any machine if you're tired, half-asleep, groggy, hungover, sick, or not paying full attention. Stop yourself before you shoot yourself.

Your gun is not cleaned or lubricated correctly – We've all seen the ads where guns are buried in mud for three years and still work fine after just a quick wipe with a silicon rag. Okay, probably true for many models, but you need to keep yours clean, dry, and properly lubricated.

Having your gun out without being in the low-ready or ready-to-fire position – Out on target, you know you should have your finger off the trigger until you're ready to fire. In the low-ready position, your finger should also be off the trigger until you're ready to come up to the firing position.

Stop calling them accidental discharges and know that they are always negligent discharges. Know your equipment and keep it well-maintained. Keep your barrel pointed away and keep your finger off the trigger until you're ready to fire. Assume your gun is always loaded and you will not have to deal with a discharge you didn't plan and safely initiate.

CHAPTER 7

WEAPONS RETENTION SKILL-BUILDING

If you carry a weapon, then there is the potential of finding yourself in a situation where you must fight to keep it. When carrying a weapon, a foundational responsibility is to maintain affirmative control and prevent it from being taken away. This includes storing and securing your weapons to avoid theft, accidental loss, or misuse.

Weapons retention is historically taught as a physical set of sequenced moves to prevent a bad actor from reaching, grabbing, and obtaining your firearm, and ultimately killing you and others. Firearms retention should be a training approach that is part of your Concealed Carry lifestyle. A common theme throughout this book is that the Concealed Carry lifestyle is so much more than just strapping on and carrying a gun.

When carrying your weapon, and really during every aspect of your daily life, it's essential to recognize that there is the possibility of losing or having to fight for your gun. Losing one's weapon either through negligence or from violence can have horrible and worrisome outcomes. A core carrying responsibility must be to maintain positive control at all times and to recognize that this as always an important responsibility.

Our 3 A's (Awareness, Avoidance, and Action) have a special place in this chapter. There are bad people who would like to obtain your gun. Ideally, if you are Carrying Concealed, the bad guy should never know you are carrying unless you present a bunch of "tells."

Tells are body language-based signals, given off through your actions, gestures, and movements, that tell people who can interpret them that you are carrying a gun. Examples of tells include patting your gun or checking or repositioning/adjusting your holster. Another tell is known as printing, when your weapon is observable by its outline against your cover clothing.

Carrying a gun presents an opportunity for someone to acquire it. Awareness should drive you to not present obvious tells, and to have an on-going understanding that losing your weapon simply cannot happen.

Avoidance follows Awareness. We can lose our guns by being forgetful or careless, such as leaving it behind in a restaurant, or more commonly in a toilet stall, or after removing it to be more comfortable. Avoidance is supported by properly positioning your gun on the same side of your body, every time, when you are out and about. Avoidance is seeing someone approaching or watching you from nearby who could present a threat. Simply stated, Avoidance drives us to not be surprised by the actions or activities of others, that would ever allow a threat to see, access, or grab or even pickpocket your gun, as might happen in a crowded bar.

A critical vulnerability to be disarmed presents itself when a situation occurs that requires you to pull your gun to defend yourself or others. This situation is always about time and distance: drawing from your holster at the right time with a safe but effective shooting distance. If the offender gets too close and is able to grab your gun while you are attempting to protect yourself, a duel for your life is suddenly in full engagement.

Your survival is now based upon who has the will, practice, and determination to win. Survival at this point requires a true test of your skill, fighting skills, grip strength, and mindset to win. Weapon retention is one of the least practiced skills of people who live the Concealed Carry lifestyle. Let there be no doubt in a wrestling match that your life depends upon your ability to regain control of your gun and to stop the person who is trying to take it, by fighting back, fleeing, or firing.

There are three phases of weapon retention: while carrying, after drawing, and off your body (at rest or in storage.) We will stipulate that weapons off your body should be properly stored and secured so as to be unobtainable by others. For the remainder of this chapter, we'll discuss weapon retention while carrying and presenting when unholstered.

While your weapon is holstered and in a situation that brings you into close contact with a bad person, the goal is to keep your weapon secured in your holster until you are able to safely clear the distance around you and stop your attacker. Depending on how you carry, inside or outside the waistband, ankle or shoulder holster, your ability to keep your gun secure might require different types of defensive practice. It's easier to keep your gun secure when it's inside your waistband in the appendix carry position, than when it's outside the waistband at the 3 o'clock location. Your gun already secured in your holster requires you to keep it in that holster while turning sharply away from the reach of the bad person.

We'll share a few examples, but it's critically important that you take the time to practice techniques with an UNLOADED and safe weapon or, preferably, a blue or red hard-plastic training gun. Never practice gun retention drills with a loaded gun. Although our examples will cover just a few carry situations, the principles of knowing your retention methods, practicing, and being prepared to fight back and protect your gun at all times, is shared across the types.

The basic retention techniques are: take affirmative control of your gun by pressing it hard into your holster, widen your stance, and spin your gun side away from the attacker. Although some holsters have retention release locks, preventing your gun from leaving your holster still requires you to have control with your hand securely on the grip. A number of issues will now surface: Is the attacker simply just reaching for and grabbing your holster or is he grabbing, striking, and kicking you in an attempt to weaken you? Once the offender attempts to access your weapon, you are truly in a duel to the death. Grab, squat, and turn away repeatedly in an attempt to get away from the offender, but know that this may not be enough. Use as many hand strikes, elbow strikes, or head-butts as you can do until the bad guy breaks loose. At some point, you may be driven to the ground and your survival skills become critical at this point.

Here are some additional self-protection points to keep in

mind. If there is one attacker, you could likely face two or more. If you go to the ground or are knocked down, you could be kicked or further struck, and your head is vulnerable. If you are knocked down by more than one attacker, work to create time and distance from those attackers. Work to get away and keep them away so you can safely clear your weapon and shoot to stop the attackers. Any grab for your gun should be considered life-threatening.

We suggest that you quickly grab and attempt to control your weapon with your gun hand, and with your non-gun hand, you pull your backup fixed blade knife and strike one or more vital points on the attacker. This will hopefully drive the offender off enough to allow you time to pull your gun. Not many offenders will want to keep reaching for your weapon if they receive immediate impact near their faces or the arteries or nerve bundles in their arms. The purpose of counter-attacking is to create time and distance so you can safely pull your gun and stop the attacker. This is preferable to prolonged wrestling to free yourself from the attacker.

Each of these two concepts requires frequent practice to assure the most expedited means of creating time and distance from your attacker. With this said, the greatest tool for maintaining time and distance is your Awareness and Avoidance skills. Staying aware and avoiding situations where you can end up in a duel for your life provides a far higher success rate than not being aware and falling into a threatening situation.

The only two hands on your weapon should be yours. If someone standing in front of you reaches forward and grabs your gun, then step back and jam the weapon forward and quickly retract it to break their grasp. A key to protecting your gun is to avoid letting others near it, and if they are to get ahold of it, to break free far enough to provide you with a clear opportunity to fire in order to suppress any attack on you and your gear.

If you carry a gun, a key responsibility is to safely keep it holstered. You must develop and practice weapon retention concepts. While you wear it, hold it, store it and set it aside while at home, a public bathroom, or any place while not wearing it or properly storing it. Practice awareness and avoidance skills to create time and distance from attackers. And, when all else fails, you must have already practiced your ability to fight in retaining it from an aggressive attack to obtain it. Practice techniques to break away, stun your attacker, and create enough time and distance for you to clear your weapon to protect yourself. It takes practice-practice-practice.

CHAPTER 8

DEALING WITH STREET PEOPLE

As a decent citizen and a careful Concealed Carry member of our diverse society, your goal in life is to avoid violent conflicts first and then settle them to your advantage if that's not possible. There is no value, legal or otherwise, to being a bully or the primary aggressor in situations where you could've avoided the whole thing. This is not to say you should let aggressive or predatory jerks kick sand in your face (Google the "Charles Atlas Dynamic Tension Bodybuilding Course" and the accompanying cartoon "The Insult that Made a Man Out of Mac").

But when you are away from the relative safety of your home and out among the population, there are various humans who roam the streets who often fall into three categories: Yes – Maybe – No People.

The distinction between the three is easy and clear: Yes, people are mostly polite, cooperative, and helpful; Maybe people will often do what is best for them, maybe they'll be nice or maybe they won't, depending on how selfish they feel; No people are rude, uncooperative, self-centered, and predatory. It is this last group that gives us pause.

Yes people don't drink too much at the bar and rudely bump into you as they are leaving. Maybe and No people do this and the No people will slam into you and start a fight because that's what they feel entitled to do. Maybe and No people get into road rage situations frequently, and No people start them and try to finish them with violence. If you guessed that our jails and prisons are filled with mostly No people, you are correct. Your goal is to identify the Maybe and No people, by sizing them up early and correctly as you pass them on the streets or the roadways, and avoid them as much as possible.

There are a lot of No People out there, roaming around in various categories, including Gypsies and gas station and parking lot scammers, who approach you with some phony sob story about needing money for gas, baby formula, prescription medications, or some other bogus reason to distract you while one of their pals quickly goes through your unlocked car for things to steal.
Gang members dwell in every large and small city and come in many ages, races, and size. The so-called "shot callers" are the ones who will ask the "wannabes" or "pewees" to engage in risky and violent criminal behavior to get them money and prove their allegiance to the gang. This includes carjackings, retail store and restaurant robberies, street muggings, and drive-by shootings, where you could get targeted or hit just walking or driving by.

Then we have two types of crooks, one quite common and the other, fortunately for our society, pretty rare. This would be the disorganized, unsophisticated crook and the organized, sophisticated crook. The first is the type of dipstick who leaves his wallet on the teller counter during his unsuccessful bank robbery attempt. The latter is the guy who steals a 2018 black BMW 765li and swaps the plates from another not-stolen 2018 black BMW 765li and drives that car for a year without anyone ever looking at him twice.

Disorganized crooks are irrational, stupidly spontaneous, and dangerous because they are emotional about their crimes. Their use of violence is sporadic, because they are often afraid of being arrested or killed during their crimes. They scream, "All you motherf____s on the ground!" when they rob a convenience store (one they came into two hours before, wearing the same clothes, just without a mask). They stagger from crime to crime, mostly to feed drug habits or to get enough walking around money so as not to have to get a real job. Cops catch these types of guys all day, every day.

Organized, sophisticated crooks are professional in their habits, motives, and methods. While they are rare, they exist and are smart enough not to draw attention to themselves while they plan their capers and execute them. The organized jewel thief doesn't come into a jewelry store with a large crew and have them start smashing the display counters with hammers to get the loot. He tails the jewelry store salesmen to a restaurant, pops the lock on his trunk when he's inside eating lunch, and drives off with his sample case filled with $250,000 worth of diamonds.

Professional crooks get caught too; it just takes longer. They use violence too, in lethal ways, against civilians and cops, so as not to have to go back to prison. They will shoot people who get in their way.

Our defense against both types of crooks is the same:

vigilance and always Carrying Concealed.

Depending on the type of city where you live, the most common group of street people that you may encounter are the homeless. If you live in a rural county area, without many services, then your chances of running across homeless people are of course less likely than if you live in a busy urban city. If you live in or near San Francisco, Oakland, Los Angeles, Dallas, New York, or Chicago, you've probably already seen the homeless problem in this country up close and way too personal. This population, once it switches from being Yes People to Maybe or No People, can be difficult to protect yourself from. Many have untreated mental illness, which can make them confused, fearful, agitated, aggressive, and in the worst case, "crazy strong."

Some of them meet the legal criteria created by the states for the police to take them to a mental hospital for diagnosis and treatment: they are a danger to themselves (suicidal), a danger to others (violent or homicidal), or what's called "gravely disabled," meaning they cannot care for their own safety in public. In these cases, the cops will take them to a mental health facility (whether they want to go or not, which often leads to a mass of police bodies piled on top of them until they stop wiggling around. This is often caught on camera by concerned and teary-eyed citizen do-gooders, who think the police are intentionally trying to harm these people, instead of getting them the help they desperately need.)

Many homeless have drug and alcohol problems, which makes them unpredictable and cyclical in their behavior – one minute buzzed and quiet, the next minute roaring-drunk angry.

The No People category of homeless can be predatory, stealing from people, breaking into cars, homes, and businesses, and preying upon other homeless or you, as you cross their paths. The worst of these types can be psychotically dangerous because they don't care about their behavior around others as they steal, mug, or sexually assault whomever they encounter. While most homeless people are fairly docile and comply when told by cops, security guards, or business owners to move along, the predatory types are firmly in the No People category and they won't, without starting a fight.

But while all this is true about this population, it's important not to stereotype or value judge your encounters with every homeless person you see. You can't paint them with the same brush.

This reminds us of taking a Logic class in college as part of a philosophy credits requirement: "All blue jays have blue feathers. This African parrot has blue feathers, so it must be a blue jay. Therefore, all birds with blue feathers are blue jays." This kind of "logic" is often applied positively and negatively toward homeless people:

"All homeless people are violent, drug and alcohol-addicted, and mentally ill."

Many homeless advocates – including Steve's good friend Ryan Dowd, the Executive Director of Hesed House, want to remind us that not all homeless people are dangerous, crazy, or drunk. It can help us all to rethink our encounter with those homeless who are not in the No People category. This complex human and societal issue requires us to have more knowledge and even more empathy.

Ryan Dowd started volunteering at Hesed House, an

Aurora, IL homeless shelter when he was 13. He thought it was a good way to meet girls from his school, only to learn they didn't sign up on the same sheet as he did. He went anyway and is now the Executive Director of the facility, which serves hundreds of people per night, as the second largest shelter in the state. Along the way and over two decades, he has learned a lot about homeless individuals.

He wrote a book about his experiences of seeing people living and coping at their near-worst. Only jail, prison, or being on the verge of death would seem more difficult to experience for most people who are not homeless. Most of us take our living circumstances for granted and could not ever imagine losing all of our relationships, sources of income, and housing options to where becoming homeless would be ever possible. And yet, as Dowd can attest, after talking to so many of his clients, the line between who is homeless and who is not can be quite fine.

Dowd has written a new book, *The Librarian's Guide to Homelessness* (American Library Association, 2015), specifically for library staffers, who clearly encounter the homeless regularly at their facilities. His book offers his years of insight and dozens of practical tools for the library folks, but his words serve as an entrance into a world few people understand, or may not even care about. As such, his book is useful for non-library people, like cops and social workers, as well.

He offers these statistics about this at-risk, highly-stressed part of our population:

National estimates are that 20 to 25% of homeless people are mentally ill. Of those 70% have personality or other psychiatric disorders: bi-polar, depression, paranoia, borderline, antisocial, schizoid, delusional, psychotic, or even a mixture of these). Many struggle with undiagnosed autism disorders. Many cannot learn from their repeated mistakes and are constantly in conflict and rude to nearly everyone who tries to help them because they cannot control their behavior during normal or especially stressful interactions. About 40% of homeless people struggle with alcohol abuse and 25% with drug abuse. On any given day in the US, 22% of the known homeless population are children, 40% are women, and 35% are families.

Homeless individuals, says Dowd, often have traits, ideas, and characteristics that are similar to ours and yet widely different. Based on his long observations of the people who use his shelter, Dowd suggests many homeless:

Grew up poor. (Often over many generations.)

Speak differently. (We use a "formal register" with strangers or authority figures; they use a more "casual register.")

Have a smaller vocabulary. (Limited education hurt their development as communicators. Simple words and clear questions or instructions to them work best.)

Pay more attention to nonverbal cues. (They really read into body language, vocal inflection, tone perceptions, and volume.)

Argue differently. (Their "anger ratio" is quicker and stronger, meaning they start loud and get louder, without much warm-up.)

View respect differently. (They see it as earned, through fair, humane, and consistent treatment, not shouting, force, or punishment.)

Look at time differently. (They don't have much more than a 24-hour time horizon. Beyond tomorrow is a long time for them.)

Value relationships. (They are highly protective of their peers. They share lots of information with each other: safe public places; fair or mean employees in government agencies; fair or mean security guards or police; where to get free food, clothing, support, which shelters to go to.)

Value their possessions. (They have an understandably strong emotional attachment to the stuff in their bags; it's often truly all they have in this world.)

Look at space differently. (Every room they are in is the same as any other room and is to be used the same way, no matter where it is or who else is there.)

Are funny. (They use gallows humor and can see the comedy in their existence.)

Have experienced more trauma. (This includes repeated exposures to physical assaults, sexual abuse, evictions, abandonment, random or targeted violence, brain injuries, arrests, job loss, and relationship losses.)

Are in more danger. (They cannot always protect themselves – especially women and when homeless individuals are asleep. This population has a lot of accompanying and untreated PTSD problems.)

Want to look scary. (Looking like a modern-day version of Charles Manson, says Dowd, is an intentional protective device to keep predatory people or violent homeless people away from them.)

Have had their IQs lowered. (Their education often stopped early and their life on the streets has hurt their capacity to learn.)

Are habituated to punishment. (Their usual and near-daily punishments – getting kicked out of a public place or threatened with jail - are not much of a deterrent to their behavior. Dowd says, "Homelessness is often the culmination of repeated punishment failing to change behavior.")

Have less self-worth. (Most homeless people have almost none after six months of living on the streets and shelters, and having to resort to begging to survive.)

Are treated like crap more. (Just about every non-homeless person looks down on them, literally, as they sit below normal human eye level on the sidewalk all day, asking for money. Their self-esteem fades to nothing soon after starting that process.)

Trust people less. (Their behavior and life circumstances have caused them to be abandoned by family members, employers, landlords, co-workers, friends, spouses, partners, or their children.)

Value fairness. (They hate being singled out for punishment for rules that others get to break.)

While it's not required that you actually walk a mile in the shoes of a homeless individual to fully understand the complexities and difficulties of their lives, Ryan Dowd's insights are a useful start to help you see them as human beings in crisis. Maybe you decide to volunteer at a shelter like Hesed House? Maybe you send some money to a shelter like his (www.HesedHouse.org) or in your city?

Maybe you just make real eye contact and offer a nod of empathic support to the next homeless person you see?

CHAPTER 9

BELLY BANDS AND POCKET HOLSTERS: IT ALL DEPENDS ON YOU

Holsters of many makes and models, used for various purposes.

We most likely have a holster for every gun type and carry situation and probably have enough in boxes to start a second-hand holster store. We can't open a gun magazine or visit a gun-related website without reading or seeing the next great carry method.

Over the years, we have selected, changed, and changed again our weapons of choice, going from 9mm to .40 to .45 and back to 9mm, large frame double stack to single stack weapons. The debate over what type of weapon and magazine capacity to favor should be centered on the mission purpose and your budget. Need a heavier round for penetration or a frangible to avoid over-penetration? It's a good starting question. Matching weapon purpose with means to carry for primary use, backup use, and your need for extra magazines requires consideration regarding your clothing and depth of concealment. Your attire (business versus casual, for example) or the type of gun fit versus how you want to cover it, will drive what type of holster(s) you select.

One carry situation might include a primary and secondary weapon and spare magazines for each. Or you could go with a "synced weapon plan," carrying the same weapon that uses the same mag for primary and backup carry, like you'll find with a Glock. Or you could use the larger capacity mag from your full-size pistol or the smaller mag if you prefer one of the subcompact models.

Further items on your EDC (everyday carry) list could include a straight-edge or folding knife, a mini flashlight, a medical first-aid kit, an ASP expandable baton (check your state for the legality of defensive sticks), OC pepper spray, and your cell phone. In time, your belt and (the changing nature of your) waistline - and especially the impact on your lower back - can easily become overloaded.

Depending on where you need to go and how you are dressed, your carry method may start as a trial-and-error experiment in finding the right solution. We like to train and practice towards more extreme scenarios, but since we teach executive, police, and personal protection courses - and believe in the Boy Scout motto of being prepared - we lean toward the obsessive side of preparation. Being caught shorthanded, without the right gear once and you'll vow to never be underprepared or wrongly-equipped again. We have colleagues who practice Concealed Carry with a .380 pocket pistol loaded with its 5 or 6 rounds and they are perfectly happy knowing they have their weapon with them and that's all they feel they will ever need. To each his or her own.

Our belly band holster experiences found us under-estimating the size and the match for our weapons, spare mags and our (apparently increasing) middle-section girths. Too-tight belly band garters can impair your breathing, generate a lot of heat and sweat, and create reholstering concerns. Once we found the right size for our weapons and our waists, we still never seemed to be able to use one comfortably. We did find a few lower-slung and looser belly bands for use with shorts and Hawaiian shirts that provided comfortable carry, however, the getting ready and donning the gear became a distraction that quickly outweighed the benefit of the holster.

With pocket holsters, our challenge was finding the right holster for the weapon system we felt comfortable carrying. What we found was that a holster that securely held our small-frame weapons presented a challenge for us to draw, clear, and fire without multiple actions that took our eyes off the threat. Have you ever had your phone in your pocket, while you were seated and buckled up in your car, and had a call come in? It's a clear and present danger to try to get into that pocket, from the seat-belted, seated position. Getting past the restraints and clearing the gun safely out of your front pocket can be a safety issue, especially under stress.

The good parts about belly bands and pocket holsters are that they give you the ability to discretely carry a weapon into places without being noticed. Since they don't imprint much, if at all, you can carry your weapon most every place you go. The not-so-good parts of belly bands and pocket holsters are actually more plentiful: limited size choices for your weapon, fewer rounds to carry, more troublesome to uncover or draw in stressful situations, and finding the right comfortable carrying situation can take a lot of time and expensive purchase to get the right feel and fit.

However, belly bands and pocket holsters do present an opportunity aside from their challenges to use as a backup carry method. Going back to our favorite US Navy SEAL saying, "one is none and two is one," means that if you have to carry small, having two weapons is almost always better than one.

Our experiences with belly bands and pocket holsters has shown us there are many good carry solutions, but they are not our first carry choice, based on our body shapes and the weapons we prefer. That said, we have pals that can comfortably carry and draw from a belly band or pocket holster with great speed and efficiency.

In the pursuit of finding the right carry method matched to our styles, we have found IWB (inside waistband), OWB (outside waistband), and ankle holsters (under your pant leg, of course) seem to work the best for us. What we have done is to alter our weapon choice based on the weather and the need to match what we wear for our social or professional activities. Because we adjust our carry methods to seasons and activities, our situational-based thinking and training allows us to practice and create efficiency using those three basic carry styles.

Many ranges do not allow you to draw from a holster or from concealed carry, either at all or without a Rangemaster supervising you. We advise you to find an indoor or outdoor range that does allow you these draws, because starting your shooting practice by picking up your pistol or revolver from a bench is not how the real world works.

With vigilance, you can find a range that will allow you to wear, test and train with varying holsters and carrying methods. Carrying Concealed requires consistent practice, situational or "What If" thinking, and regular, useful training. Borrow different holsters to test from your shooting pals (since they probably have a lot of spares sitting in boxes like us.)

If you watch, or even better, participate in practical shooting programs this offers an excellent way to see how champion shooters wear and operate their carry methods during match shooting scenarios.

As one example, the IDPA (International Defense Pistol Association) is one of the many shooting programs that promote safe, everyday carry, realistic training scenarios, and offers an excellent opportunity to field test your holster and carry preferences.

CHAPTER 10

PRACTICING IN THE DARK TO SHOOT WELL IN THE DARK

If you have had military service, then you are familiar with the need to be able to assemble and disassemble your weapon in low light or no light conditions. This exercise of putting your rifle or handgun back together in darkness was meant to stress you and remind you that bad things happen most often at night. (Being constantly yelled at by an intense man with stripes on his sleeves may not have made this exercise any easier.)

If you've not done this type of practice session before, then now is the time to start. With safety being your first order of business, prepare your pistol and/or revolver, rifle or shotgun, by moving all ammunition to another room. With the gun completely unloaded, find a dark room (your bathroom, maybe?) and set up shop. Practice taking your firearm apart and putting it back together.

Check your success and then practice using your

speedloaders to reload your revolver (using empty brass, not live ammo, of course). Practice pulling your (completely empty) magazines from your belt case and loading and unloading them into and out of your pistol. You should be able to do all this in simulated low light or no light conditions. Now do it with the gloves you would typically wear in cold weather times of the year.

In a perfect world, you should be able to load, unload, disassemble, and reassemble any of your firearms in dark or darkening conditions without having to use your flashlight. It's tactically important to do all you can to protect your night vision if you have to engage with a bad guy at night or the pitch-black hallways of your house.

While it may be difficult to simulate clearing jams, stovepipes, and double feeds at home (and if you can do so, remember not to use live ammo in your setups), that skill set is just as important. You need to remember the steps to Tap-Rack-Clear-Bang when you can't see very well.

Some of you may be thinking, "Why do all this? I have a flashlight mounted on the frame of my gun, along with a cool laser light. I even remember to take my small tactical flashlight with me when I grab my gun in low light situations." Good for you on all counts. But, frame-mounted lights and lasers can fail, get damaged, fall off, run out of batteries, or some shooters can even forget how to turn them on in moments of high stress. You can forget to recharge your tactical flashlight, drop it and break the bulb, or forget to bring it. Do your low light training work.

Practicing at the range in low light can help a lot too. Bring your darkest sunglasses to the indoor range and go through the three flashlight positions with your gun: LAPD-style, FBI style, and headlamp style. The LAPD method puts your strong hand with your gun over top of your support hand/wrist holding the flashlight. The FBI method has you hold the flashlight in your support hand, over your head and as far away from your body as you can position it. The headlamp method has you hold your flashlight in your support hand and place it against your left temple (if you shoot right handed, and right temple if you shoot left-handed), so that as you turn your head, your eyes see what your flashlight sees. Each has its advantages and disadvantages.

Practice, practice, practice turning your attached gun light (and your handheld flashlight) on and off, in the proper laser/light sequence, so you can manipulate the buttons without looking at them or fumbling around for them. If you have a combo laser light and flashlight mounted to your gun, you must know (and that means memorize, under stress) the series of buttons you have to push to get the laser only, the flashlight only, both lights, and then neither of them. You should practice these important sequences during your dry fire sessions. Strive to make these button pushes smooth, so as not to jerk or move your gun off your target.

Today's tactical flashlights are small, tough, adjustably bright, and rechargeable. They can pack a lot of lumens in a small size, but that same small size makes them easy to drop under stress. The days of the three C-Cell battery black metal foot-long combination flashlight and head basher are over. You shouldn't use your flashlight (or your gun) as a club, except in a life-threatening emergency and even then, civil and criminal trial juries won't like the sight of you using a big metal tube up against someone's head because they all get a reflexive flashback to the Rodney King situation.

There are plenty of articles out there that vehemently opine that you should only use your light for short bursts, and then move after you do. It's not bad advice, but it shouldn't be carved into stone advice. "Crooks will shoot at your light, so if you are holding it center mass or near your head, you'll get shot there." Maybe. The Fog of War makes all absolutes not so absolute. As Mike Tyson so eloquently puts it, "Everyone has a plan 'til they get punched in the mouth." Sometimes you might need to hold your ground and can use your light to completely blind and disorient your attacker. Getting 1200 lumens beamed into the ol' rods and cones can make it hard for anyone to find you and shoot back.

If necessary, use your voice commands like your flashlight: say what you need to say and then move. Better to use your light to identify both your target and your background, then to shoot blindly into the dark and risk missing, or hitting not what you aimed at.

One theory, as espoused by Steve's police tactical mentor and well-known gun writer, John Morrison, is to get more comfortable operating in total darkness. If you've been blessed with good prenatal nutrition and decent night vision, use it to your advantage by relying less on your flashlight and more on being able to move, reload, and sight your pistol or shotgun using whatever light is available, inside or out.

CHAPTER 11

HOW TO BE YOUR OWN BEST WITNESS AT A SHOOTING SCENE

A big part of "being prepared" is the pre-planning for the when-all-else-fails situation and you're involved in a shooting. We are often surprised when we talk to new CCW trainees and other Concealed Carry people to find out they either do not have a plan, or they figure the bad guy will be shot and everything after that is going to be okay. It should not be a shock to realize that if you are involved in a shooting situation, you can expect some real challenges that last anywhere from months to years afterward. You survived the incident, the bad guy is down; you saved your life and/or the lives of others, but stand by. Your stable life is about to get dicey, unsteady, and shared through the media and the criminal justice system.

Our "what if" must include surviving the aftermath of the shooting and the expected onslaught of questions from the police and prosecutors, along with public attention.

We have talked about our practice of "Awareness, Avoidance, and practiced Action." We've also discussed the value of scenario-based training, having the proper gear, and knowing your holsters, weapons, and ammunition. What must you do to help yourself when your shooting incident creates a shooting scene with an investigation? This is as important, if not even more important, than all your other preparations.

First, when law enforcement officers are involved in a shooting, they too are put through a rigorous investigation. Your involvement in a shooting will get a similarly thorough investigation because you're the shooter and they likely do not know anything about you or the situation. How you present yourself will go a long way toward helping yourself survive the experience, legally, emotionally, and physically. Conversely, your lack of preparation will go a long way in harming the success of your post-incident investigation. The Carrying Concealed lifestyle begins and ends with the proper survival mindset.

There are a plethora of reasons to be prepared for a post-shooting event: you and or others may be injured; you are likely to be upset, considering you were just in a situation where the only course of action was to shoot the offender; you could have been shot or killed during this ultimate self-defense decision to protect yourself; and you may feel unsteady, upset, or on the verge of shock, for even days afterward.

This period of high emotions is not the time to develop your post-shooting plan. Further, just about everyone there will have cell phones, cameras, and access to social media sites, as will the local media. There should be no doubt that pictures, videos, and sound bites, about what you did or didn't do, will be digitally captured at all times. At this moment of crisis, you have a role and how you play your role can help or harm the outcome of the incident.

Law enforcement arriving at a shots-fired situation only know what was transmitted via their dispatch, who will probably have received one or more 9-1-1 calls (from you or others who heard or saw what just happened). Shots-fired police response with likely causalities will have responding officers in a heightened state of action-ready until the scene is controlled. You will be the person who has shot someone, and the police need to bring quick control of that scene. Until that control is obtained, they may not initially see you in a good way. For the safety of officers and others, the police will be direct in assessing and ensuring that the threat is over. You standing there with a weapon in your hand, over a body, will certainly cause the officers to have their weapons out and pointed at you until they understand and take control of the situation.

Every action you take after the shooting should be considered important to support your claim that the shooting was sadly necessary to save your life or the lives of others. Your prime concern should be your future legal survival and you should keep in mind how important your actions and words are. Once you get your criminal defense attorney to the police station, you will want to assist the officers or detectives in clarifying the incident and to provide the specific elements of the situation for the investigation necessary to clear you. You will be in the spotlight and every action you took will be analyzed, verified, and compared to what the forensic evidence at the shooting scene has revealed.

Since you elected to live the Concealed Carry lifestyle, the reality of this situation has to be considered. Now, during this dynamic set of moments after the event, with shattered nerves, you will face questions, potentially inflated allegations, and you will have legal concerns. You will need to be the one to help yourself, by having a criminal defense attorney with you and by telling the truth. If for example, you kicked the bad guy's gun out of his reach after you shot him, tell the police exactly how and why you did that.

In our various chapters about making a gear list, we discussed the need to have your CCW permit, your defense attorney's phone number, and your insurance card with you. Legal support and insurance programs (like from the US Concealed Carry Association or the NRA's Carry Guard) for Concealed Carry members provide specific recommendations and guidelines to follow should you be involved in an incident. The insurance and recommendations are to assist you during the difficult events that follow your shooting incident.

Have no doubt that you could possibly face criminal charges and need legal assistance as soon as you get taken to the police station for questioning. Once the legal issues are settled and the shooting is determined justified, then civil charges could follow, as the surviving bad guy or if the dead bad guy's grieving family sues you. There is a realm of possibilities that will have costly impacts that insurance and legal aid could assist with. This is why in our preparation, the awareness of these possible outcomes must be considered for those living the Concealed Carry lifestyle.

Following the recommendations from organizations like the NRA, USCCA, and other insurers helps position you for the best possible outcome from a difficult event. As the shooter, you are the best first witness to the event. Your statements and actions will be viewed, recorded, and noted by witnesses, victims, and responding law enforcement, and then further scrutinized by prosecutors' civil attorneys, judges, and insurance investigators.

What you say and do are important parts of your justification and explanation of self-defense. Most CCW insurance carriers advise you that right after calling 9-1-1, you are only to say "This person tried to kill me," "I am willing to sign a complaint," "He had a weapon," "These people saw the attack," and "Officer/Detective, I will cooperate 100% but first I need to speak to my attorney."

Remember, this event is a highly-emotional time for everyone on the scene or who arrives at the scene, including the paramedics who may have to treat you or the bad guy you shot. But because you should already be practicing "Awareness, Avoidance, and trained Action" means that, though you will likely be upset, you will also be aware of the environment, other witnesses, and important facts that prove your defense. You have a smartphone too, and it would be a good idea to quickly capture pictures or video of the area, the people standing around, people parked in their cars, or other items, statements, or proof worth remembering.

Or, activate the voice recorder on your phone and quickly describe the surroundings, what you see, how the event evolved, and how you had no choice but to step into harm's way. There are those who will suggest that you should not take pictures, videos, or record any information because it could be used against you. Your defense attorney can give you advice on this, since whatever you create will be subject to discovery at a criminal or civil trial. If this was a legally-justified shooting, and you're not covering up any wrong-doing, then you need to ensure the data is captured quickly and electronically, so you won't have to completely rely on "eye" witnesses (who actually saw what happened) or **"ear"** witnesses (who may have only **heard** what happened), to accurately report what was going on. Know that everything becomes important and will be used to help or hurt you. The prosecutor in your city or town may not be your friend.

If court proceedings or other civil actions are required, the truth you tell and the facts that can be verified will have to fully support your decision to take the life-saving action you choose. It will be your recollection of the environment, weather, lighting, use of force situation, and those who were around you that will help bring the most accurate details for the investigators as they review the incident.

Unless absolutely necessary to continue to save your life from active threats, you should not have your gun in your hand when the police arrive. You should secure it in your car or bag or re-holster until they come, depending upon the continuing ability of the person you shot to harm you. The police will take it as part of their evidence collection. If you are not sure the police were called, you should call them. But this is the time to make sure you have the facts ready for 9-1- dispatcher and the responding police.

The facts the police need are much like what a film director would need to film this segment if it were a movie being reviewed. What was the scene and setting, who were the actors, and what was the action sequence?

The sad worry about all of this is that we as Concealed Carriers and law enforcement officers will have to deal with a post-shooting process that at times will seem unfair, frightening, and outright unnerving. This is why we need to pre-think this concern and have a plan and process to deal with the madness. You must be your own best witness in a situation that you will feel is out of control. You are a responsible, Concealed Carry, law-abiding citizen. It's your duty and your right to protect yourself.

CHAPTER 12

PTSD: DEALING WITH THE AFTERMATH OF YOUR SHOOTING

If you ever have to shoot someone, even if you did the safest, legal, and right thing - your emotions will take you on a roller coaster. Expect to feel doubt, shame, fear, anxiety, sadness, guilt, and even anger, as in, "Why did that bad guy force me to pull the trigger?"

In the coming days, weeks, and months, you may experience up and down mood swings and hypervigilance, where you can't seem to turn off your need to protect yourself or your family. You may have sleep problems and nightmares, intrusive thoughts, no appetite, digestive problems, low sex drive, headaches, not much energy, and just a general body ache and fatigue, which doesn't seem to want to go away.

You may want to cope with alcohol and sleep medications, which are not good for you separately and can be fatal when taken together. Don't interfere with your mind and body's natural reactions to this type of trauma with chemicals. You can expect to feel awful, then better, then awful again, all in the span of a day or a week or a month. Know this now and if it happens: these are all ***normal human responses*** to an ***abnormal situation***. You're not going crazy; you've just experienced life-threatening, life-changing stress. How you will cope with this going forward is the big question.

Many people who have been in shootings experience both ***triggers*** and ***anchors***. Triggers happen when you experience a related or even unrelated part of the event; something you see, hear, smell, taste, or touch can be a trigger. Examples include driving by the scene of the shooting and feeling anxiety; hearing gunshots while watching a movie, or loud noises around you, which triggers your startle reflex; or even something simple as the smell of your gun while cleaning it. These can become anchors, as they trigger the same negative mind-body responses for you again and again.

You could get triggered by news stories about your shooting, or being in the courtroom and seeing the guy who attacked you. Often the one-year anniversary of your shooting can become a trigger for you to re-experience the stress of that event, all over again.

The need to get qualified, licensed, empathic therapeutic help is now just a given after a shooting event. We've proved the value of therapy for survivors of wars, horrific national events, or local disasters. The therapy process has evolved and improved because of the significant post-trauma support work that has helped our soldiers, police officers, firefighters, paramedics, and dispatchers get back to normal lives, even after they have been exposed over multiple times to incredibly bad things.

Besides just psychotherapy and cognitive behavioral therapy (often called “talk therapy”), therapists trained in EMDR (Eye Movement Desensitization and Reprocessing) can get great, lasting results for their clients with PTSD.

Even if you think you’re plenty tough, tough guys and ladies need help too and it should be a sign of strength to get help for your internal wounds, just like you would do if you had visible wounds. Referral sources for help with your PTSD symptoms are readily available from your family doctor, pastor, or your health plan.

Just like you should keep your criminal defense lawyer’s business card handy, you need a list of available mental health resources too. If you know any cops or firefighters, or a veteran with combat experience, any of them might be able to make a referral to a skilled clinician with experience in PTSD treatment.

Your employer may have an EAP or Employee Assistance Program provider you can access for free. EAP services are confidential and refer you to specific therapists who can help you address the many personal and professional stressors that may have arrived because of your shooting.

There are some distinct differences between the various mental health-related caregivers. Licensed psychologists provide therapy. Psychiatrists are medical doctors who can prescribe anti-anxiety or anti-depression medications (as can your family doctor). Licensed Marriage Family Therapists (MFTs) can provide therapy, like a psychologist. The key is to choose a provider who has real experience working with post-traumatic stress disorder (PTSD), not just general life problems. If you’re looking for help after a shooting incident, it really helps to work with a therapist who has been trained in police psychology, military PTSD, or similar support of first-responders.

If you're a churchgoer, you may get help from an experienced pastoral counselor at your house of worship. There are pastors who understand that sometimes, you need to take a life to save your life, and it's not a sin in God's eyes to protect yourself and your family, as all good shepherds need to do.

People thinking about going to therapy often misunderstand confidentiality and the therapy process. It is not the job of the therapist to get you committed to a mental hospital, get your guns taken away, or ruin your life. They are supposed to work with and for you. The only exception is if you say you want to kill yourself or someone else and you refuse to go for crisis treatment at a hospital. For those situations, they are bound by the ethical and licensure requirements for their states, to either get the client immediate mental health care and/or tell the people who were threatened.

A shooting can bring on life-changing trauma and it's best addressed by a combination of three supportive areas: talking in confidence with family or friends who really care about you; meeting regularly with a therapist who specializes in PTSD work; and lastly, the passage of time, which serve to blur the intensity of the situation. What was painful soon after the incident can create intrusive thoughts and nightmares, but this will start to lessen in intensity over the passing weeks and months after your shooting, but only if you talk it out. Holding bad things inside is a classic male trait; we want to be perceived as a tough person who can cope. Too much of that can lead to a negative life outlook, severe depression, and suicidal thoughts or actions.

One important step is to document the timeline and steps you took in your shooting event, down on paper, as soon as you can. Your recollection of the shooting changes over time. To protect your psyche, your brain may play tricks on you, leaving out or changing certain details it doesn't want you to cope with until later. It's common to have tunnel vision and/or tunnel hearing during these events, where you can't remember how many rounds you fired or even hear the sound of gunfire around you. You may only recall new details in the days, weeks, or months after the shooting. Writing down what happened helps you organize in your mind what took place; you can fine-tune your recollection of the accuracy of the event as the days and weeks go by and your memory improves, and it helps you to capture your version to support your testimony in a civil or criminal trial. This document should be given only to your criminal defense lawyer, so it is protected by attorney-client privilege.

Clint Eastwood said: "A man's got to know his limitations." If you ever get to a point where you are so depressed, or you have so much survivor's guilt about what you have done, where you consider suicide, you must get immediate mental health help. You need to have the courage to ask your family to safely lock up your guns, and take you straight to your family doctor, the emergency room, or an in-patient mental health hospital. Nothing that you experienced in a shooting event is ever worth taking your life as a result. No one in your family or your friends will ever say that your suicide was the right thing for you to do. Get help and save your life and your family's pain.

It should be no sign of weakness to get help for your internal wounds. Experts who study these events talk about the Power of Hardiness, or the ability to bounce back, to cope, to be hardy, to see a better future beyond the traumatic event, and not let it ruin your life. Getting into a shooting is rare and life-changing. But it's an event ***in*** your life, not the event ***of*** your life. Lots of people have survived these incidents involving the correct and legal use of their firearms. With professional legal help, talking with mental health professionals, support from family and friends, and the passage of time, you will too.

CHAPTER 13

PISTOL, SHOTGUN, OR CARBINE CARRY CHOICES

If we were to Google, "What's the best pistol, shotgun, or carbine choice?" you could expect to get a couple million hits filled with expert opinions, recommendations, and suggestions. We're going to cut that list down by providing some of our own opinions and recommendations based upon a few important criteria.

The ideal firearm is one that you can and will carry and use. Aside from what round is best, holster type, the magazine size, wheel gun or semi-auto options, shotgun or carbine choices, the weapon you can and will use should be your primary weapon. Each of us has our favorites, based on our experiences, but what works for us may not work for you. The weapon you train with the most, whose operation you know well, the one which you can grab/draw and use in an intense, stressful situation, should be your primary. It's our recommendation that even if you only carry one type of gun, you train with a variety of weapons: open and enhanced sights, carbines, shotguns, revolvers, and semi-automatics.

Assuming you are well-versed in various weapon platforms, your choice of carry can broaden to include matching your choice to the type of threats you might face. You should consider your neighborhood, the street environment, the types of weather, your normal clothing, and how to protect your family. Living in rural America, I might not make a five-round 2-inch .38 revolver my first choice when I could have a 300 Blackout Pistol with a thirty-round magazine or two. How about if you live near the water in a warm climate, where shorts and t-shirts are the norm? Carrying a Glock 43 9mm with a spare magazine in a belly band holster might be your best run-around weapon.

Cities that you live, work, visit, or travel through have to be considered; some are safer than others. (Steve is from Baltimore, enough said.) If you live in a neighborhood with lots of acreage or miles between the homes or those that are located far from first-responder services, you're likely to need more protection than just a revolver. Aside from their hunting and recreation weapons, rurally-located legally-armed citizens should have gear based on their operational space. Mike prefers the combination of carbine and pistols. Some shooters have adopted the pistol caliber carbine (PCC) weapons to match their pistols, for example, a 9mm pistol and PCC that use the same magazines. Those living in vertical high-rise cities are likely to be more pistol-centric while at home or out and about; they might have a shotgun for the home and a pistol while on the move.

Much of our lives seem to be spent on the road, commuting to work, recreational traveling, and vacationing. This can create a Concealed Carry challenge for most of us. Aside from the fact that Concealed Carry laws vary from state to state, we must also worry about weapons access, storage, and security. For IWB (inside the waist-band) appendix carry, sitting with your large-frame, compact, or sub-compact against your belly, with a seat belt on, for multiple miles, could start to get painful. If you needed to quickly draw your gun, it may not be the quickest move while seated and seat-belted in.

So the best place to carry that pistol while driving might be in an anchored holster, between the seats, in the middle console, or in your go bag. This creates a situation where you store your weapon in one place while walking about, and another while driving. All is good until the road bio (bathroom) break at the fuel stop is required. Where does that IWB appendix carry gun go during a quick sit-down in the bathroom? Believe it not, many have not considered where they should place their gun while using the bathroom.

Not that this is enough to worry about — what about the rest of your belongings locked in the vehicle at the local stop-and-rob? Yes, bad guys know you may be in the bathroom and know they have a short time to burglarize your vehicle. If you have a carbine, personal items, or other things you care about, how are they locked down and secured in your vehicle? How can you make your vehicle the least attractive target in the lot?

These points we are raising are meant to generate thought and consideration that surround the idea of what you'll carry. The real consideration of what to carry may begin with what you can and will use but should also be about what's right for you as a legally-armed citizen in the operational spaces you will occupy 24/7, regardless of where you are and what you're doing.

When being prepared, one is good and two is better with regards to carry guns. Reliance on a single weapon for multiple purposes puts you at risk of not being prepared if and when you experience a mechanical failure. Having five rounds is better than not having any but wouldn't having twenty or thirty be better when cornered in your home waiting for the police to help? Isn't having a flashlight better than no light when needed? Or having a knife as a tool to cut a seat belt or fight off an attacker to save your life? Preparation requires serious in-depth thinking about what to have for where you will be at every phase of your daily life. This is part of the lifestyle of Carrying Concealed for the purpose of your self-protection.

For home defense, we all need a strong physical security system, a process to remain safe while first-responders are en route and, when all else fails, the means to legally protect yourself with a weapon you've trained to use.

Mike is a fan of pistols and a carbine. His neighbor has a shotgun. Mike's co-range coach has a carbine, shotgun, and a pistol. Each of us came to our individual setups based upon our experiences, backgrounds, and training comfort. While Mike has been a long-time pistol Concealed Carry guy, he competes with the carbine and pistol combo. His co-range coach is a three-gun competition shooter. His neighbor has limited weapon experience and feels his shotgun will protect them.

The decision about which weapon to own or carry requires some real thought around your activities. Assuming you have embraced the Concealed Carry lifestyle, have the right weapon for the right needs and be sure it's properly purposed to your daily lifestyle. We should all be capable of effectively using a pistol, carbine, or shotgun, and have practiced in situations that match our potential use scenarios. Each should be aware of the effective range and capabilities of those three weapons. Everyone should consider how they would be used in your 24/7 lifestyle. How will they be stored, carried, and secured? Once you determine your selection by your usage needs, practice, and then practice some more.

CHAPTER 14

MODELING YOUR CONCEALED CARRY RESPONSES LIKE POLICE USE OF FORCE RESPONSES

Just like a cop on the stand after a police shooting, here are some potential questions you might get asked by a prosecutor or plaintiffs' lawyer. These questions could come at you as a result of being arrested after your shooting, even if you did everything legally, or during your time on the stand for your criminal trial (with the hope that you will be a witness and not a defendant), or at the table at a civil trial deposition.

As we have said before and will say again, the time to think about the answers to these questions is after you have a Concealed Carry insurance policy on file and the name of a skilled criminal defense attorney already in your wallet.

The prosecutor, and especially the bad guy's civil attorney (hired by him or his family if he didn't survive his encounter with you), will want to call the bad guy "the subject" or by his last name – as in "What did Mr. Smith do after you shot him?"

You and your lawyer should counter this by always referring to him as "the attacker," "my attacker," or "the man who attacked me." Civil attorneys (who are not always very civil to people they're opposing) will attempt to humanize him, as if he was on his way to his momma's house or his weekly visit with the Pope when you just wandered by and "gunned him down."

Anticipate your answers to these:

Was your response to this situation reasonable?

This is a common and court-tested word that asks the question, "Was your use of force or deadly force reasonable, within the context of the situation?" In other words, did you have other options or was that your only recourse. This question comes up a lot in civil trials. Was the employer reasonable when they fired the employee for stealing? Was the one neighbor reasonable in asking his other neighbor to trim the trees that hung over into his yard? The opposite of being reasonable points to things like targeting, revenge, or picking on the other person. In your situation, the question can be answered by saying, "Yes. My conduct in this situation was reasonable because my attacker was armed and meant to put my life or my family's life at risk due to his actions. I considered all my options – escape, hide, avoid, deter – and none would have worked to save my life or the life of my family. He left me no other choice."

Were you injured prior to or during this event – how, where, and how severely did it limit your mobility or ability to escape, get help, or protect yourself in another way besides using your gun?

This is an important distinction and one you need to articulate with facts and accuracy. If you walk with a cane, explain why that injury or disability prevented you from fleeing. If the attacker broke your wrist in the struggle, explain what happened and why you needed to protect yourself before he injured you more severely or killed you.

If you were injured, seek documented treatment at the Emergency Room or with your physician. This is not the time to be tough; if you were injured, have the paramedics take you to the hospital. Police investigators will respond as well, and can take pictures of your injuries to help confirm your version of the events. You may also want to take photos over several days after the incident, to document bruising.

How significant were the height and weight differences between you and your attacker?

Juries like to see differences. The 240-lb. cop will have a hard time justifying why he kicked the 160-lb. suspect in the head during an arrest situation. If you are large and fit and muscular and your attacker is a skinny meth tweaker, juries and prosecutors will all want to know why you weren't able to overpower him with your bare hands. You need to articulate why your gun was your only choice at that moment.

What were the apparent age, physical fitness, strength, or conditioning differences between you and your attacker?

Again, back to differences. If your attacker was a lot bigger, younger, more fit and muscular, and significantly stronger-looking than you, you need to explain each of those differences to a prosecutor, civil lawyer, or jury. "His 20-inch biceps and the `Kill the Police' tattoo on his face made it clear to me that I would not survive a hands-on fight with him." Don't embellish your answers but be clear as to how you thought you could win the confrontation without using deadly force.

Do you have martial arts training? How much and how long ago?

This is another hot-button issue for lawyers and juries. If you have a black belt in some martial art and you used a firearm to stop the threat, your actions will be called into question. This is largely because lawyers and juries watch way too much TV and movies and have seen their action heroes on the small and big screens kick guns out of the hands of the bad guys for too many years. If you have martial arts experience, don't over-sell your ability and don't lie, since it may be possible for them to verify your skills. But don't be forthcoming with that information if you're not asked about it.

Did you believe your attacker had martial arts training based on his words, fighting stance, or posture toward you?

This question actually helps you, by illustrating the attacker's desire to start or continue the fight. Tell them if he said, "I'm into mixed martial arts and now I'm gonna smash your face into the curb!"

Did the subject demonstrate skills with a weapon?

If your attacker had a knife and he kept changing stances, hand positions, and making different grip selections, which would suggest he has some familiarity with a higher level of knife fighting.

What is your level of training or military experience with a handgun, tactics, fighting, or close-quarters combat?

Again, don't oversell your military qualifications or training or gun range proficiency. Tell the truth, but leave out that you were your gun club's shooting champion five years in a row. All that will do is inject doubt in a jury's mind that you should have "shot the gun out of his hand" or "shot him in the knee," like people see actors do on TV and in the movies.

When was the last time you fired your gun?

This is a critical question to help you and your attorney prove your competence with your gun. If you belong to a gun club or range that keeps records of your trips, pull that information, along with any classes that you have taken that were taught by certified instructors. Carry your CCW card and be able to provide proof that you have maintained your firearms proficiency and eligibility requirements in your county and/or state.

Did your feelings about the subject's race or youthfulness play into your decision to shoot him?

The answer to this leading and loaded question should always be a firm "No." His race and age had nothing to do with the actions I had to take. He threatened my life and that was all I focused on."

How many actual or potential suspects were near you?

This is a useful question for you to answer because you can articulate that you were fearful of being attacked by the bad guy and his friends. Juries need to know that violent crooks often operate in pairs and larger groups.

Did your use of alcohol or illegal or prescription drugs harm your decision-making abilities?

This is a classic question if the confrontation with the bad guy took place inside or outside a bar. This is also a good reason not to drink any alcohol if you're carrying concealed in public. If the police tested you at their station for drugs or alcohol – and that's not always a given – a clever prosecuting or civil attorney will jump all over your positive test results as the reason you shot without considering the consequences.

Did you believe the subject was under the influence of drugs or alcohol? How did that affect your decision-making or his?

Another good area for you to point out to your examiners that at the time you encountered him the bad guy looked high on meth, alcohol, or some other drug that made him act crazy, irrational, and unwilling to listen to your commands to stop.

Did you believe the subject to be mentally ill? Based on what behaviors or statements he made?

Like with drug use, bad guys can come in all shapes and sizes when it comes to their mental illnesses. Mentally ill people can be both fearful of other people and fear-creating around other people. We've all seen videos where it took five big cops to handcuff one "crazy strong" mentally ill suspect. Describe your attacker's behavior as being a danger to you and others in a way that heightens your sense of fear that they were out of touch with reality, soon to be violent, and destined to hurt you if you did not protect yourself.

Paint the picture with your statement. If the attacker was

acting like a crazy man, describe it: "His face was red and he was sweating and screaming at me, with spit coming out of his mouth. He was waving his arms around, his fists were clenched. He was yelling and saying gibberish things I couldn't understand. But then he said he was going to stab me to death when he pulled out his knife. I heard that part clearly."

What is the nature of the encounter initially? How did it progress? Over what time span?

These can be trap questions, designed to point the holes in your story, especially when there are moments when you had the opportunity to flee, get help, call the police, or protect yourself in a way that didn't involve using your firearm. Describe what happened, in the order of your activities and the bad guy's, and make certain you show how the situation escalated based on the bad guy's behavior, that forced you to shoot.

Was the subject non-responsive to your requests to stop or stay back? Did you warn the subject before you fired?

If you had any dialogue with the bad guy, say specifically what happened. This is a good reminder not to say things like, "Stay back or I'll blow you motherf---ing head off." Witnesses remember these statements and it doesn't look good to a jury if they think you wanted to be the next Dirty Harry.

Did you have the ability to flee or call for help?

A hard question to answer. Accurately describe why you couldn't do either until the scene, the situation, and you were safe.

How many times did you fire your gun and why? Did you reload and why?

We recall a recent California police shooting where a City Council member asked the Police Chief in open session, "How many times should officers shoot at someone? What is the number of rounds they are allowed to fire?" Since there is no real answer to either (and both questions are flawed and only designed to stir up controversy with the public), the Chief answered correctly by saying, "There is no designated number of shots to fire in a deadly force situation. Officers are trained to fire until the suspect is no longer a threat to them."

Answer honestly, since the ballistics and forensics reports will tell the real truth, and explain how and why you were trying to "stop the threat that you believed would end your life." You could be completely truthful and say, "In the stress of that life-changing moment, I really don't know how many shots I fired. I only discovered it was three after the police examined my gun." It's quite common even for cops not to know how many shots they fired in a gun battle.

If you reloaded and shot fifteen more rounds into his unmoving corpse, you will have some problems explaining why.

Did you offer first-aid to the person after you shot him? Why or why not?

One answer might be to say, "I ran to my car or went inside my house and got my first-aid kit and did X-YZ with it to try and save my attacker's life." Another answer might be, "I called 9-1-1, described the situation to the fire/paramedic dispatcher and waited for them to arrive from a position of safety." Or, "Since I had no first-aid kit or any formal first-aid kit, I called 9-1-1, described the situation to the fire/paramedic dispatcher and waited for them to arrive."

How soon did you call 9-1-1 after you stopped firing your gun?

A loaded question designed to make you look like a horrible ogre if you didn't call 9-1-1 within seconds of the shooting. If there was any delay at all – while you looked for cover, reloaded, or protected your family, explain why. Know that your 9-1-1 call is being recorded and may be played in court. Be as calm as you can on the phone and explain what happened in brief and not full detail: "He attacked me with a knife or a gun and I was afraid for my life, that he would kill me or my family, so I drew my gun and fired at him. I'll be waiting for the police." (Fully describe yourself and say where your gun is at the moment.)

Did you move or remove any evidence from the scene?

A dangerous question. Tell the truth. If you kicked the bad guy's gun away tell the cops what you did.

What did you not tell the police upon their arrival?

Read this question again, carefully. It suggests you omitted details in your first version to the responding police, versus what you're saying to them now. Know your story and stick to it, every time you tell it, during interviews, deposition, or a trial.

How or did the situation go from "no-shoot" to "shoot" to "no-shoot" to "shoot"?

This is another hard question because the answer is yes, every potential shooting situation goes from no-shoot to shoot to no-shoot, and all in a matter of seconds, not minutes. Describe your decision-making process, in detail.

Self-Protection Themes:

1. You feared for your life or the life of your family.
2. The attacker left you no reasonable choice but to fire.
3. You are heavily outnumbered by multiple suspects, who could have been or were armed with deadly weapons.
4. You feared being disarmed and killed with your own gun.
5. The attacker advanced despite warnings by you, in front of witnesses who could also have been injured or killed by the attacker.
6. The attacker advanced on you in the presence of an armed or unarmed security guard.
7. The attacker advanced even though he knew the police had been called.
8. To the police: "I thought he was going to kill me, so I defended myself. I will answer more of your questions, but I want my attorney present."
9. Describe your state of mind: "I had just finished working a ten-hour day" or "I was going to the market for ice cream for my family" or "It was very late at night or very early in the morning and I couldn't see him until he was right on top of me."

Future Testimony Warnings:

Never say you were planning to "shoot to kill." Always say, "I had no choice except to shoot in order to stop the threat to my life. I fired my weapon until the attacker was no longer a threat to me or my family."
Don't shoot at or from moving cars unless you are certain you will be killed if you don't.
Always consider the background behind him, your potential accuracy, the potential for your ricochets, and the proximity

of innocent people, especially if you are likely to miss one or more shots.

Never give more than one verbal warning if an armed attacker crosses your already-defined physical boundary. Quickly draw your "shoot" or "no-shoot" red line in the sand. If he crosses it, fire and be ready to completely explain why.

Explain yourself fully by writing down or tape recording exactly what you remember, over the span of several days after the shooting, as your memory improves. Be certain to discuss this with your defense attorney, since things you create (statements, diaries, journals) could become discoverable in court.

(Our thanks to San Diego County DA Commander (Ret.) Wayne Maxey, for his exceptional knowledge and contribution to this chapter.)

CHAPTER 15

CONCEALED CARRY IN LOW AND NO-LIGHT SITUATIONS

Of all the Concealed Carry gear we have lugged around and used, none has been more useful during all times of the day and night than our flashlights. It's our experience that of all the gear licensed Concealed Carriers have with them, the flashlight is the most likely item to be left out. Illumination is our friend, and can be used for self-defense, personal protection, area searches, and to just create a greater sense of security. Lights provide a beam of truth in unknown shadowy situations.

There is not one of us who has not needed a flashlight during a project. And most likely not one of us who have wondered what that noise was in the dark and nervously used whatever means possible to search around that corner. Darkness can create anxiety and nervousness and in stressful or threatening situations, it further burdens your ability to establish control over a situation or attacker.

Imagine waking at 0230 in the morning to a loud noise near your front door, as your spouse pushes you awake from your groggy sleepy fog. “What’s that?” is what you both think or say. You grab your weapon, slide out of bed, and creep towards the bedroom door, searching with your ears in the dark to discover the source of what’s making you shake. You freeze as you hear another sound downstairs in the dark. Knowing now that it’s not your imagination that someone is walking around downstairs you slowly walk forward in the dark towards the noise, hoping your pounding heart won’t give you away. You reach the top of the stairs. Looking down you barely can see, but clearly hear shuffling steps. You hold your breath, holding your weapon in front of you, pointing into the darkness, when the stairway hall lights come on, nearly blinding you, and you see a person standing not ten feet in front you. You point your gun at the chest as your just-home-from-college-daughter says, “Hi Dad!”

All that makes noise in the night is not bad, but not seeing or knowing the source because of poor lighting and your inability or failure to illuminate what’s ahead of you creates a dangerous situation that could lead to a disastrous outcome.

The power of flashlights is that they remove the shadow of doubt or concern over what we can't see. Illumination helps in identifying avenues of escape or exit, reaches into and lighting the dark corners, assures friend or foe, and makes the inky darkness less frightening and stressful.

To prepare for situations that may happen each of our vehicles have flashlights with spare batteries. Near each door of our houses and bedrooms, we have flashlights charged and at the ready. Our range kits and go bags have flashlights with spare batteries. Mike's tactical carbines, shotgun, and pistols have mounted lights. (Steve is more of a shotgun guy and not a rifle guy.) Our experiences over the years have simply shown us that not having lights creates more stress than having adequate lights.

It is without hesitation that we suggest that low and no-light weapon training is probably some of the best range training you can receive. The ability to understand the power of illumination both offensively and defensively provides a strong enhancement to your shooting skills. Light helps you understand the shooting space as well as how to control your apprehension by removing darkness.

Flashlights as tactical support gear for Concealed Carry help by: identifying threats or intruders; momentarily disorientating or scaring intruders; and revealing clear paths for exiting or evacuating. Additionally, tactical lights with metal frames and bezels can serve as your striking tool if someone gets too close.

But what flashlight should you carry? It depends. The more lumens your light has the more power it has to both white light an area and temporarily blind your attacker. (Don't discount the power of blinding the bad guy. He can't grab, hit, or shoot what he can't see.) The ideal light for defensive carry will have at least 300 lumens, be big enough to fit in your palm to use as a striking tool, and be small enough to carry conveniently.

The next flashlight consideration is durability and reliability. Should it have an LED or regular bulb? Should it have replaceable or rechargeable batteries? We look for strength and power that over time that will work every time we need it. Over the last couple of years, the power and reliability of LED lights have increased. Issues that have shelved our gear include damaged bulbs or fast battery burnout rates. Therefore, our current carries include strong lumen LED lights with the ability to have replaceable and rechargeable batteries.

Not one of us hasn't experienced the frustration of needing a flashlight, but not being able to find one. Most of us have also experienced grabbing a light only to find the batteries dead or near dead. Many of us have a flashlight with a bad bulb that takes up space in the junk drawer because we don't want to or know how or where to get it fixed. Some people just grab their smartphones and use those notoriously weak lights to assist themselves. You need reliable, durable, and properly placed lights that you can get to and use when you need them.

Tactical weapon mounted lights

Tactical position and carry lights.

Mike says, "Interestingly, the majority of my light use has been during the day. The second most used time is shared between early morning, around 0600 and in the evening, up to 2200. The heaviest use of flashlights during the day is for clearing or searching rooms, hallways, storage areas, maintenance and utility closets, cars, planes, boats, and other transportation types.

"One of my students in an executive protection course once complained early in the class after I pointed out that he was not properly equipped to perform his assignment because he didn't have a flashlight. He argued that it was daytime and assured me that he would have his light at night when it was dark. Not being one to highlight a student's weakness during training, I replied, `As you wish and good luck today in your tasking.' It wasn't an hour into the advance drills of checking and clearing rooms and vehicles that this student was attempting to use his smartphone to light up dark areas. Communicating, taking notes, and using his GPS, all without a flashlight left our unprepared student with mounting challenges with his missing gear and ability to be effective.

"Later in our daily debrief we discussed findings in our advance team preparation, including issues in utilities, vehicles, and gear readiness. I asked our unprepared student to share his findings, and to rate his effectiveness and readiness. To his credit, a lesson was learned and now this once-unprepared student is an effective leader and as far as I know, always has ample lighting even during the day."

Many of our tactical lessons learned come from our mistakes and the uncomfortable feeling of not having the right tools for the job. Low to no- light scenarios are a given and will happen to each of us. Which light and how you carry or access your light is a personal choice. We lean toward being over-prepared, as we always have small LED easy-to-carry flashlights as well as weapon-mounted lights.

The days of the big black nightstick flashlight with the large six D-Cell batteries have been replaced with high-powered LEDs run from a single AAA battery. Mike can't resist teasing someone in the training environment who uses their smartphone flashlight to clear a house or an area of darkness. Take a low-light training class at your range and spend some time looking up and reading about low to no-light shooting situations and how they were addressed. You will see being prepared to fight at night will reduce your fear, misery, and stress.

CHAPTER 16

30 STUPID AND SEMI-STUPID CCW MYTHS (AND THEIR REALITIES)

1. You can shoot a guy on your property, especially if he is across your doorway.

   (You can shoot anyone who is threatening your life with a deadly weapon or who has the ability to kill you using any means. You cannot shoot anyone, on your property or off of it, in your home or on your patio, half-inside and half-outside your house, unless they have the ability to injure or kill you. A burglar carrying your TV away from your house doesn't put you at risk of death. Don't shoot.)

2. Pointing a gun at, or better yet, racking a round into your shotgun, will stop most bad guys.

   (While the shotgun rack move sounds great on TV and in the movies, there's no real evidence it deters anyone who wants to shoot you. You should only point your gun at what you plan to shoot. Keep your gun in your safe, your holster, pointed safely toward the ground at your side, or in the low-ready position, until you need to fire it. We don't point guns at people to scare them or for show.)

3. Glocks rarely need cleaning or lubrication.

   (Despite their awesome marketing efforts, with Glocks covered in water, mud, and who knows what, all machines with metal moving parts need to be cleaned and lubed. Read the Glock instruction manual that came with your gun, download it online, or watch YouTube videos for the best ways to clean and oil your Glock.)

4. Don't leave rounds in your magazines too long; you'll wear out the springs.

   (The opposite is more likely. Taking your rounds in and out of your magazine too often – not at the range, but just to have something to do – is what can wear out the springs. Still, if you buy factory mags and not cheap knockoffs, you shouldn't have issues with worn springs.)

5. You don't need to aim a shotgun.

   (You had better never say that to the police, a prosecutor, or a civil attorney. We aim every firearm and we take care about where the round goes when it leaves whatever sized barrel. We use our training and experience when operating a shotgun; we don't just spray and pray.)

6. You don't need a holster for a pocket gun.

   (True, if you want to make that gun more likely to get stuck in your jacket or pants pocket, fall out in public in an embarrassing way, or shoot yourself as you grab for an uncovered trigger.)

7. You don't always need a holster; just jam your gun under your belt.

   (Same as with the pocket gun, moving in public without a holster risks your own injury, a negligent discharge, dropping your gun on the deck, or maybe even getting disarmed by a smart bad guy who sees you don't know how to do Concealed Carry.)

8. You don't need to carry extra rounds.

   (Even cops, who are supposed to be well-trained, fire and miss in gun battles. One round won't stop most bad guys right away, even in the head or heart. No worse sound in the world than your revolver falling on an empty chamber or your pistol cycling back to reveal an empty mag. Guns fail and magazines fail. Better to have a backup for each, handy and nearby.)

9. You don't need an Everyday Carry (EDC) bag.

   (Yes, you do. Consider your EDC bag to be your lifeline when life goes from calm to horrible. Opinions vary as to what are EDC essentials, but we like things like these: a flashlight and batteries; knife; extra rounds in your mags or speedloaders; a compass; a tourniquet and pressure bandage for chest wounds; a glow stick; extra cash and a credit card; spare phone charger; a granola bar; a bottle of water; a foil emergency blanket; a butane lighter; some paracord.)

10. Bugout bags are for doomsdayers, preppers, and worriers.

    (Maybe before 9-1-1 you could make this argument, but certainly not now. Consider the value of having a Bugout Bag in your car, at your office or worksite, and certainly in our home. Fill it with the contents of the EDC bag above, except times ten and on steroids. You'll need enough water, food, cash, toilet paper, toiletries, guns and ammo, knives, and heat and shelter resources to keep you alone and/or you and your family, safe and protected for at least a week. It's not just bad guys storming our walls, but weather incidents and wildland fires that can put you on the run. Stop putting this on your "I'll Get Around To It" list and make it happen.)

11. You won't need a first-aid kit at the range or anywhere else; rely on the paramedics.

    (This might be true if you live in a town where your fire department and ambulance companies are fully-funded and fully-staffed. Many people live in places where this is not the case and the response time ranges from concerning to excessive. As such, while we love our first-responders, it's up to you to be ready to provide first-aid to yourself or others within the so-called critical "Golden Hour." Take a first-aid class, which should include tourniquet training, CPR and AED training, and basic first-aid blood stopping and bandaging. The leg you save at the range or in the streets could be your own, a family member's, or a stranger. Either way, a necessary skill for all who live the Concealed Carry Lifestyle. Re-read our chapter on the value of combat tourniquets.)

12. You don't need a flashlight in the daytime.

    (Some daywatch cops have said this, only to go to calls involving creepy and unlit warehouses, attics with burglars inside, or into other dark areas where using the flashlight option on their iPhones just won't cut it. Get into the habit of having a flashlight in your EDC bag so you won't have to add it in every time the sun goes down.)

13. The police and the District Attorney will be on your side if you get in a shooting.

    (Maybe and maybe not. They may think either you're a good person who did a good thing with your gun or a good person who did the wrong thing with your gun, but they are going to analyze your motives, actions, and decisions in ways you didn't think were possible. Prosecutors and DAs say they are on the side of the law and the search for an application of equal justice, but we know that's not always true. As your criminal defense lawyer should have already told you, the cops are not always your friends, so until your lawyer gets there, keep your storytelling to a minimum: "I feared he was going to injure or kill me, so I defended myself. I'll wait to speak to my attorney before I answer any other questions."

14. It's okay if people see the imprint of your gun under your clothing or a bit of your holster under your coat.

    (Since we already know we live in a country where roughly half the people hate people who own guns and about half the people like or don't mind people who own guns, be careful to not draw attention to yourself in any public place because of carrying your firearm. The goal when you leave your house is to never show your holster, any part of your gun, or even any imprint of your holster or gun. Dress accordingly and keep what needs to be covered, covered.)

15. Bad guys won't try to disarm you if you're holding your gun on them or they see it in your holster.

    (Admittedly this last part is a rare possibility, but we've seen it happen, especially in bars or other crowded, confined spaces where a slick-fingered crook sees you're carrying a gun and basically pickpockets it off of you as he goes jostling by. In the disarming scenario, real crooks, who have been to jail and especially prison, actually practice gun takeaways with each other. Whether they want to try this risk behavior with you or a cop who tries to arrest them at gunpoint, know that they may be quite skilled at these maneuvers. Rule One: Always keep your gun holstered and covered until you need to draw it. Rule Two: Never get close enough to a bad guy who you are pointing your gun at to be disarmed.)

16. You can carry your semi-automatic pistol with an empty chamber, because you'll have time to load it when you need it.

    (If you have the ability and motor skills, under life-threatening stress, to first remember to draw your gun and then jack a round into the chamber, just prior to firing, then you're a whiz kid. Most people don't have that kind of pre-trained sense, so the next sound they hear in a real gunfight is a horrible click as the striker-fired hammer falls upon emptiness. We've known cops back in the day, who kept their duty guns in this highly unsafe position, either with their revolvers (see right below) or their pistols. With this highly-unsafe approach, you have to add additional and unnecessary steps into a stress-filled environment. Who says you can remember to do this? And why should you have to?)

17. Setting up your revolver so the hammer falls on to an empty chamber is a good way to prevent accidental discharges or to keep from getting shot with your own gun if you get disarmed.

    (See above. Just no good reason to do this, ever.)

18. You won't be able to put on your own tourniquet if you get shot.

    (First, yes you can, and second, you had better be able to do this. Lots of people in combat situations have saved their own lives with tourniquets, when they've had the proper training and time to apply them. Tightening a tourniquet on one of your wounded extremities, and packing your own bloody wound are things you need to know how to do if you are going to carry and use a gun. Study our chapter on the value of first-aid skills.)

19. You can keep your finger inside the trigger guard even if you're not ready to fire.

    (No. Put "accidental discharges" into Google or YouTube and see how many times people had their fingers on their triggers just seconds prior to the round going off into the ground, or someone's body, or their own foot or leg. Cops tend to do it a lot, even though they have been supposedly trained not to put their finger inside their trigger areas when they are running after a suspect, searching a room, or arresting a bad guy. It's a horrible and potentially deadly habit. Just because you see TV and movie cops doing it, doesn't mean you should.)

20. If the police are in danger, they will want you to help them with your gun.

    (Uh, maybe and maybe not. There are no hard and fast rules on when to help one or more police officers struggling with an armed, mentally ill, or drunk/stoned suspect and when to simply be a good witness and watch wait for more of them to arrive and help their brother or sister-officer. We've seen stories on the Internet where law-abiding citizens with legal Concealed Carry permits intervened and saved the lives of cops who were shot or being shot at. Those are both phenomenal and rare. Better to be asked to help, either in a serious situation where you can first quickly and safely tell the cop – without distracting him or her – that you're armed and can help them, or in a situation where it's obvious the cop is getting his or her clock cleaned and they will thereby welcome the help. Otherwise, standby to standby and don't; add to their problems.)

21. You should tell your friends and neighbors that you're CCW in case you need to protect them.

    (Sure, that is if you want them calling you at all hours for every domestic dispute, loud party, bullied child at school, or worse, home invasion burglary. Best keep that info to yourself to avoid lengthy arguments with anti-gun types or to keep your house and guns from being ripped off by your friends' creepy friends, who keep their ears open and eyes peeled to steal from people they know, because it's just easier.)

22. It's okay to leave your gun in the glove box or center console while you're driving or you leave the car.

    (Two problems here: It's hard enough to get your gun out and on target in a hurry when it's in a holster on your ankle, under your shoulder, or on your waistband, and if you leave your gun in your glove box or center console, there is a good chance it won't be there when you get back to your car 15 minutes or five hours later. Carrying Concealed means we carry.)

23. Big ammo and a big gun will protect you better than little ammo and a little gun.

(More to the point: ammo that misses the bad-guy human target it was aimed at is worthless at every caliber. Mafia hit men use .22 rounds – allegedly – and it seems to work for them. You should be able to hit what you're aiming at no matter what gun or what caliber you're carrying. If that means you have to get really good with one gun and one caliber first, before you start switching models and sizes, so be it.)

24. It's okay to carry concealed if you've had a few drinks, as long as you don't drive.

    (If you get into a shooting, chances are good the cops will test some fluid from your body – blood, urine – for drugs and alcohol. In point of fact, we would suggest that your criminal defense attorney insists that they do, to forensically prove that you were clean and sober and no alcohol or no legal or illegal drugs were in your system at the time you pulled the trigger. This will prevent a prosecutor or a civil attorney from asking you on the stand: "So, on the night in question, you really don't know how drunk you actually were, right?" or "How many prescription pills would you say you need to have taken to be impaired, or don't you know?" The only way to make sure there are no drugs or alcohol in your system at the time of your shooting is to make sure there are no drugs or alcohol in your system if you have to fire your gun. In other words, it's an easy decision: Plan on having a few drinks tonight? Don't carry and don't drive.)

25. Dry-firing can damage your gun.

(No. Unless the manufacturer of your particular handgun forbids you to dry fire your gun – and always check your owner's manual – it can save your life. Perfect practice makes perfect shooting. Be safe when doing it and do it a lot.)

26. If your attacker takes a knee, you can no longer shoot him.

(Kind of a tricky statement here. Some bad guys will go down when you shoot them and stay down; others are still in the fight until they stop breathing. You can't shoot a bad guy who gives up from his knees, but there's a reason people down south call it "playin' possum." Be fully aware of when the threat to your life is over or not over.)

27. You don't need to practice at the range or dry fire once you get your CCW permit.

(No and no. Getting your Concealed Carry permit just means the real range work, classroom training, and attendance at instructor-led courses has just begun.)

28. It's a waste of time to practice with your support hand.

(Since most of us shoot with two hands – strong hand on the gun and support hand helping with the push-pull balance, positioning, and grip, we'll note that our hands and arms are often held at chest and eye level. This means any bad guys with shooting skills can also shoot at your center mass and hit one or both of your hands and arms. This means you not only need to know how to shoot one-handed, you need to need to know how to load your revolver or pistol one-handed. Both take dedicated practice. Watch some YouTube videos on the safe and effective ways some training qualified instructors reload with only one hand.)

29. If you have your CCW permit, you can clear your own house by yourself if someone breaks in.

    (Maybe, if you live in a rural community where the law enforcement is a substantial distance away and your family may be inside. Otherwise, if the house is empty, take up the best observation position near your house, to be able to see the perimeter, and let the pros arrive and do their thing. They have radios, vests, long guns, tactical training, and experience doing this.)

30. If you have a CCW permit, it's better to shoot a bad guy, rather than run away or get behind cover.

    (Back to those tough questions by prosecutors and civil attorneys who want to nail your hide to the courtroom wall. Your first choice of self-defense is to avoid the fight. Every other option will only happen, legally and ethically, after that choice has evaporated. If you have the chance to protect yourself from behind solid cover and be a good and rational witness until the police arrive, do that. Protect yourself with deadly force only as a last resort and be able to fully explain why ultimately that was your only choice.)

CHAPTER 17

THE WORLD OF POSSIBILITIES FOR GUN SIGHTS

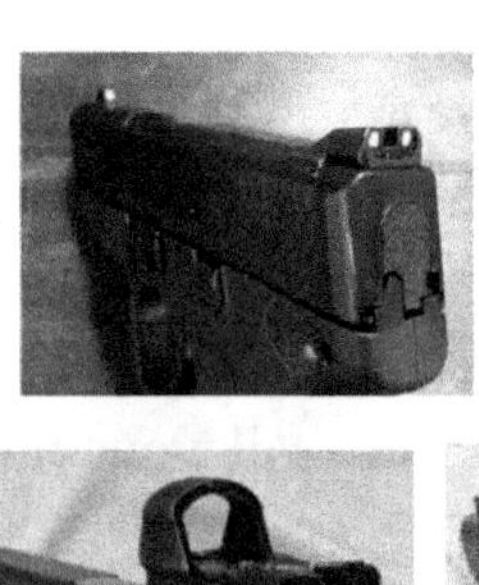
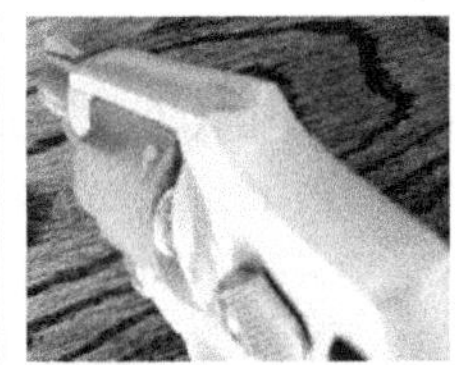

Where to begin in the world of possibilities in finding the right gun sight? Let's start with the phrase "proper purposing." The beginning of your sight search should start with the question, "For what purpose will I be using my sights?" Your selection of gun sights needs to be aligned with your purpose and your eyesight.

Mike's purposes for sight selection include: everyday urban carry, everyday field carry, home defense, tactical weapon shoots/competition, perceived shooting distances, and recreation. Over the years he has found that his sight selection has changed. Besides the vision changes we all face as we age, the ability to acquire a target and get the front sight locked in on our desired target has improved with many aftermarket sight enhancements.

Mike says, "For my everyday urban carry, my leading need is a strong front sight for short distances. The types of weapon I may carry in these settings have fewer rounds and are likely single-stack. Since I perform range drills to simulate these conditions, I focus on having a clear front sight on my intended target. Having a strong front sight is helpful. In the photo above, the far left and far right weapons in the top row both have strong front sights. There are glow (tritium) dots, fiber optics, and varying colors to assist in front sight focus.

"For everyday field carry, my leading need is an ability to sight in at longer distances with a larger-frame weapon that carries more rounds. The top row photos three and four are reflex sights, with a red dot for quick and accurate targeting at short and long distances. Reflex sights can mount on slides that are made for Modular Optic Systems (MOS). These slides are machined to accept mounting plates for varying reflex sights as shown above. Many after-market solutions are trending to support reflex sights. The photos above show examples of an MOS mount (image 2) and a dovetail mounting (image 4) for a reflex sight. Reflex sights provide fast targeting solutions by simply putting the dot on what you want to shoot versus the need for a fast alignment of the front and rear sights.

"For home defense, my leading need is to consider short-range shots in all lighting conditions. Further, my home defense plan includes the potential use of both my handguns and my carbine. For now, I have open sights for the handgun and reflex sight for the carbine. I always plan for low-light situations and have a light mounted on each weapon as well."

"Tactical training shoots and competition have opened up to duty carry or everyday tactical carry systems for competition. For tactical training and competition, I like to train with my purposed selections. However, the incentive to have a competition weapon has driven me to get a large frame set-up with some enhancements, to include a reflex sight. The ability to identify targets and move from target to target is enhanced with the reflex sight. The sight change does require some added practice, considering you have a red dot on a slide that is bouncing back with each round fired. For me, finding the red dot versus the strong front sight is a bit more difficult with the benefit being that once I do find it, the shot is more accurate than the open sights. The red dot versus the alignment of front and rear sights has the red dot leading in accuracy."

For tactical shoots and front sight, focusing on the target has many people replacing the rear marked sight to a larger fan black sight, the thought being that the rear black sight has the front more visible sight, presenting a stronger sighting solution.

Recreational shooting, hunting, or distance target shooting has shooters finding the right scope for distance. In the bottom row of photos above, we have the two bottom left images with red dot Aimpoints. The Aimpoint Patrol and Micro provide quick target acquisition and shorter distances.

The scopes provide a reach out with clarity for longer distance shooters. The scope on the bottom row of photos, far right has the scope, reflex, and laser sight combination. This combination can be mounted on a weapon to cover short to long distances with each selection tuned to a zone.

Aging and younger shooters with challenged eyesight are benefiting these days from a wide array of sight possibilities. Mike's decision to move to a reflex sight was motivated by his desire to quickly acquire the target and enhance his accuracy. (Steve will say it's because he's aging and can't see as well.) Perhaps he is correct, and others feel the same, since the USPSA (United States Practical Shooting Association) has just created an enhanced optic division for competition using reflex sights.

Aging shooters and people with poor eyesight are also

finding green dots easier to see than red. Front sights have moved from white dots to fiber optics showing red and green.

The challenge for shooters and their sight selections is the dynamic of vision. Shooters who wear corrective lenses often have difficulty finding their front sight at arm's length, as well as a target that might be feet or yards ahead of them. Of course, shooting schools and range instructors frequently suggest focusing on your front sight, with the rear sight and target being a bit blurry. Mike says, "With my progressive lenses, I found my head bobbing as I worked the sight from target to target at the range. With the reflex sight, I was able to use regular sunglasses without correction and find both the red dot and my multiple targets. Reflex sights have reduced the fatigue of focus and allow me to have more meaningful attention to the red dot and targets."

Additional sight considerations include tritium, which provides a glow for low-light situations. Mike says, "All my earlier weapons had the sights changed to Tritium sights. However, these sights have a shelf-life of about ten years. With these newer sights, Tritium sales may see a slight drop off as shooters move to fiber optics and reflex solutions."

Sight size for front and rear sights have also changed over the years. Shooters that have reflex sights or suppressors may find they need to change the front sight as recommended. A larger front sight for reflex for "co-witnessing," should the battery fail in your reflex sight. Co-witnessing is the ability to use a rear and front sight while having a reflex sight. Since the reflex sight sits higher on the slide, the need for a larger front sight exists. Weapons with suppressors require a larger front sight to accommodate for the size of the suppressor.

Lastly, the width of sights has changed to support the changes in sights. Fiber optic front sights are typically larger in width and height. The pairing of the front and rear sight is important if the shooter is simply changing his or her open sights to enhanced open sights. With a larger front fiber optic sight, you need a groove or rear sight gap to help the front-rear sight alignment.

So what sight is the best for your Concealed Carry? It depends on your purpose and eyesight. The best solution must match you, as your weapon truly needs to be aligned to you. If you have vision challenges, what's your plan if for some reason you don't have your glasses in a defensive situation? Should you consider not having your glasses, all full and low-lighting situations, and all distances as defensive possibilities? Yes, you should. Whatever you decide, the range is waiting, where you should practice your low-light and distance situational scenarios.

To practice without your corrective lens eyeglasses, sunglasses, or shooting glasses will require eye protection, but test with uncorrected sunglasses with a reflex sight. Otherwise make sure you have your glasses, and a backup pair of glasses, in every shooting situation.

With all this said, cost is also always an issue. Reflex sights and weapons set up with MOS can be expensive. Leupold Delta Pro Reflex sights are going for nearly $400 dollars. Weapons with MOS set-ups seem to cost a bit more than weapons without. Concealed Carry solutions do require thought on sights and what your carry purposes are. The good news is that each of your purposes will require range time and range time, done well, is always good. Train as you fight, since you will always fight as you have trained.

CHAPTER 18

COULD YOU SHOOT A WOMAN OR A TEENAGER (WHO WAS TRYING TO KILL YOU)?

The question above is about as straight-forward as can be. It's no secret acts of crime and violence are a man's game (and a young man's game, to be most accurate; most crooks are burned out, in jail or prison, or dead by 40). But, and it's a big exception, women can be crooks and violent ones at that. While roaming bands of female robbers seem unlikely, lots of 15 to 25-year-old women will do bad and dangerous things on behalf of their boyfriends who are robbers, thieves, general thugs, gang members, or dope sellers.

As workplace violence prevention practitioners and threat assessment experts, we have worked on threat cases involving women as the potential perpetrators. Women have killed people in the workplace and school violence incidents, not nearly as many as men, of course, but it's not impossible for the cops to respond to an incident involving a female shooter.

How about a teenager with a gun? Haven't we all seen cases around this country where pimply-faced adolescents have taken guns, rifles, and shotguns (procured from their parents' homes, who were too lazy or stupid to use gun safes or trigger locks) and killed their schoolmates or strangers at malls, businesses, and churches?

A wily old police tactics teacher said it so well, so long ago: "If you aren't willing to use deadly force against anyone who has shown the desire to kill you – and that includes women of any age, senior citizens, or teenagers – then quit now and go sell shoes."

This statement was related to something said by a police officer who was a lay pastor at his church and a deeply religious person. The officer told other officers he either couldn't or didn't know if he could (stories vary) take the life of another human being, based on his religious beliefs. You can guess that this same officer was killed in a shootout where he did not get a shot off against a killer who murdered him and another officer at the same location. Would you want that cop protecting you if you were another cop? Would you want that cop trying to stop an armed burglar at your house or an armed robber at a store you were in? With all due respect to the dead, he should have given up his badge and went into another line of work.

Our first national recollection of the possibility that kids younger than high school age could kill was after the school shooting in Jonesboro, Arkansas, where a 13-year-old boy and an 11-year-old boy shot and killed four students and a teacher at the Westside Middle School. They used rifles and handguns.

So imagine you were a responding police officer to that scene. You might have had to engage with a pair of heavily-armed killers. They already proved they could kill upon your arrival. Could you shoot a 13-year-old or an 11-year-old preparing to shoot you with a handgun, rifle, or shotgun? Your answer had better be yes, or don't carry concealed.

The point is bad people can come in all ages and genders. The chances of you coming across an armed 13-year-old bent on killing you with a gun are certainly mighty slim. But we don't live in a world of statistics and What Might Be. We live in a world where people of all ages, races, nationalities, and genders can do bad things to themselves and others, using suicide bombs, knives, and cars to injure and kill people in public places.

Having studied school shooters for 25 years, our conclusions about why they shoot up their campuses are varied. Some are bent on revenge and hate themselves and other people so much that they don't care about how many they kill before they kill themselves. But perhaps others didn't realize the seriousness of their actions. When they were arrested, their statements as to why they did it suggest they didn't think they were really going to kill people. Maybe they just want to scare them? The responding cops either negotiated with them to give themselves up or they were tackled and stopped by brave people on the scene.

But the stone-cold killers who are bent on revenge and havoc cannot be stopped with words or even pointing a gun at them. They need to be stopped with deadly force – which means do it to them before they do it to you, even if it's a woman or a teenager.

On February 12, 2010, University of Alabama-Huntsville

biology professor Amy Bishop, 44, brought a 9mm pistol to a faculty meeting and shot and killed three of her teaching colleagues and wounded three others. She was sentenced to life in prison without parole. Do you think the responding campus police and local law enforcement would have had any qualms about shooting her if she didn't give up on their arrival? We assume the answer is and will always be no.

So how might this necessity of having to shoot an attacking teenager or a female happen in the real world? How about when you interrupt three teenagers who are burglarizing your house? They are armed with knives and refuse to drop them when you point your gun at them? How about a gang member's girlfriend, who accompanies him to carjack you at a traffic light? They both have guns and try to order you out of the car? Could you shoot both in defense of your life? The answer had better be yes or they will win. Maybe she had a terrible childhood, full of physical and sexual abuse. Maybe her gangster boyfriend beats her, forces her to take drugs, and "loans" her to his other gang pals for forced sex. All tragic and too bad.

None of those backstory issues will make any difference to you if she kills you dead at an intersection. The courts and her defense attorneys will make much hay from her horrible upbringing, but that won't bring you back to life.

Our gun clubs both have a video simulation room which features dozens of computer software-driven shooting programs (called the Laser Shot program). The simulator uses a 1911-type pistol, with working grip and trigger block safeties. One of the many modules is based on the FATS (Firearms Training Systems) approach to police training, with shoot or don't-shoot scenarios. These can be fun and stressful at the same time, as bad guys jump out at you or appear quickly and you have to figure out if they are a threat and whether or not to shoot them. Take this type of training on an irregular basis if it's available at your range.

Having a concealed carry permit means you have taken on the enormous challenge and responsibility of taking the life of someone trying to kill you or your family member. Hesitating because the attacker in your sight portraits is young, old, or female could result in them taking you out. Be prepared to stop any armed threat, anytime, anywhere.

CHAPTER 19

SMALL-FRAME .45S

Does size really matter? Whether you want to carry in .380, 9 or 10mm, .45, .40, .38, .357, single stack, double stack, small or large frame, what's the right weapon for Concealed Carry? Is the caliber of the bullet more important, or the number of rounds it carries? Or does the size of the gun and the bullets not matter as much as your accuracy? Since Carrying Concealed begins and ends with a mindset, let's evaluate why a small frame .45 is a good choice for self-protection.

There exists a thought theme "shooter's choice." where many have and will not sway from their favorite round, weapon, holster, or carry position. This chapter is not intended to force you into a way of thinking or to promote a weapon brand, but rather to create a conversation about what you could carry and why.

Our "shooter's choice" involves balancing a number of variables to determine our carry. Over the years, we have learned to respect the punch of 230 grain jacketed hollow points. Mike once heard this large bullet explained as a "flying ashtray, used to disrupt an aggressor's foundation, providing an enhanced opportunity to survive an encounter." The usual debate over what is the best bullet for self-defense has bounced between 9mm, 10mm, .40, and .45 and the discussion continues. Part of this debate is the concern over how many rounds you can carry at a time. Single stack .45s range from seven to nine rounds, with one chambered. Double stack .45s can get up to 10 to 15 rounds. What you have to consider is the size and weight of the weapon you intend to carry.

The advantage of the .45 is the large grain bullet's ability to clearly disrupt an aggressor's "platform" (his stance) with enough energy to penetrate coats and clothing, and the ability to break bones. If the round is right, then how many do you need? Some will say that just a few rounds are enough because they are well-versed at shooting. Others will not feel comfortable with a single stack weapon with seven rounds plus one chambered. A shooting moment nightmare you don't want is engaging with an aggressor and running out of rounds.

Mike often carries a Smith and Wesson M&P Shield .45 with 7 +1 loaded and two spare seven-round magazines. This small frame .45 fits most of his carry situations. This provides him with 22 chances for survival. The M&P Shield is a small-frame, single stack .45 that impressed him with its ease to carry, shoot, and care for. For short-distance shooting situations under 15 feet, this weapon will send and place that 230 grain jacketed hollow point as aimed. In considering why and when to carry this weapon system, Mike's choice is about the comfort, environment, likely shooting situations, and necessary power required.

There are other shooter choices for a small frame .45, such as 185 or 200-grain bullets. Mike continues to find the 230 grain as his choice, based upon his range time with each of the other rounds. The ultimate shooter choice criteria should include your results, your range work, and the outcomes of your test shoots in various situations and settings you are likely to face. For Mike, this includes doing his own round penetration tests through objects and clothing.

With a dozen small-frame .45's to select from, the next challenge is to find your fit. Which of these small frame .45 can you comfortably shoot, care for, and train with to the needed confidence level? Over the years, we have mainly carried Glocks and feel very comfortable with the operating parameters of Glocks. We don't prefer weapons with manual safeties or decocking levers. We practice safely, so our shooting fingers are not inside the trigger well until we are ready to fire. Since we train in multiple scenarios, our comfort levels and abilities are improved without having to worry about taking extra steps to make our weapons safe or ready to fire.

Our carry choices have morphed over time and are now tied to our sense of potential shooting areas or situations. There are times our carry solutions are with 9mms, with one to two double stack magazine systems. Other times we may be outside the waistband (OWB) and will carry a double stack .45 with a single stack .45 backup. However, for frequency in shooting, ease of carry in multiple situations, and dependability, the small frame .45 is Mike's most ready-to-go carry setup. (Steve often carries his Glock 30SF, which is a compact .45 10 + 1 double stack model.)

Again, what works for us may not work for you. Several folks we train find Mike's Smith Wesson M&P Shield .45

accurate and easy to hold and shoot. It’s worth remembering the importance that the pulling and using of that .45 is a near last choice. Practicing strong situational awareness and avoidance skills, we evaluate the areas we enter. Before getting out of our cars, we look around and if there is something that looks dangerous, we avoid putting ourselves into unsafe positions. When entering a building, taking a walk, or eating at your favorite fast-food restaurant, you should know the ways in and out, and be in constant “assessment mode” to any potential safety issues. If you see something develop you will know your exit routes and should be ready to take the best one to leave.

Even if you have 22 rounds of the powerful 230-grain bullets and an accurate handgun, engaging in a gunfight if you first have a clear exit is not logical or recommended. (It will be hard to justify to a judge, jury, or prosecutor why you didn’t choose to avoid the fight if that was an option.)

The best survival case is based upon getting off the “X” and not be at a threat situation in the first place. Only when awareness and avoidance fail, should you act with practiced efficiency with the tools you train with to protect you and the lives of others.

The right weapon with the right round used in the right way is ultimately decided by your selection by plenty of shooting and testing the gun, round, and holster systems of your choice. The small-frame .45 is both a weapon and its round that complements our training and evaluation of threat scenarios. We are able to carry this weapon in many ways and feel as comfortable as one can feel about having multiple disruptive rounds at our disposal.

Smith and Wesson M&P Shield .45

CHAPTER 20

LEARN TO LOVE YOUR REVOLVER

During Steve's cop days in the 1980s, he was a wheel gun man and not by choice. This was in the days before law enforcement agencies realized the tactical wisdom and necessary firepower of semi-autos, a decision later made easier by the North Hollywood bank shootout in Los Angeles in 1997. After that incident, Glocks, Smiths, Sigs, Berettas, and Rugers began to fill the pistol gap in cop's collective duty holsters.

There are lots to choose from in revolvers today, from five, six, seven, and eight-shot revolvers, including the new 8-shot Ruger Redhawk in .357 Magnum. This bad boy weighs a whopping 44 ounces unloaded, but the 2.7-inch barrel still keeps it in the "snub-nose" family.

Revolvers still have a place in your Concealed Carry Lifestyle, especially as a backup gun, a car gun, or a (big cargo pants) pocket gun. We get that there are a lot of obvious pros and cons discussion points on revolvers, some which are valid and some which are a stretch:

Pros:

Lighter, and easier to carry and carry concealed, with a smaller holster imprint. Great for summertime Concealed Carry.

Easier for women who are not all that much into guns to carry and fire than most larger-frame semi-auto pistols. There are no hard slide pull/tight spring issues, but the tradeoff is the hard trigger pull when the revolver is fired in double action.

Excellent as a belly gun, for close quarters combat shots to the bad guy's torso when at grappling distance. Great for ankle or pocket carry and as a second gun when you need more than just your pistol or you run out of ammo or it fails beyond a tactical fix. Revolvers can keep you in the fight.

A good gun for carjackers, as long as they don't get their hands on it as you point it at them. The downside for revolvers in close quarters is they can be stopped from firing if the crook gets his hands on the cylinder. Fire faster and don't let bad people or their hands near any of your guns.
Fewer moving parts means way less jamming and ammo malfunctions – only a broken firing pin or some kind of bent cylinder or jammed barrel will stop a revolver. Unless the gun is broken or the ammo is bad, you will almost never have any kind of mechanical failure.

(Don't spin the cylinder like you're trying to be Ranger Rick or Black-Hearted Dick from the old west days. Spinning the cylinder and slapping it into the frame can damage the "timing turn" – our description of it – and make the firing pin hit the rounds slightly off-center.)

Cleaning and lubrication are a bit easier, with no disassembly necessary. It's just as important to keep a revolver clean and well-lubricated as with a semi-auto pistol.

As we have said throughout this book, it's not always about "stopping power"; it's more about "hitting power." A .45 semi-auto round is of no use to you if it misses the target.

Cons:

There is definitely more recoil because of the shorter barrel, so you have to really, really learn not to flinch when shooting it. The recoil and the longer, tougher trigger pull in the double-action mode make it a hard gun to control without practice, especially for shooters with weaker grips and smaller hands.

(To eliminate this common flinching problem, you must practice doing either empty cylinder drills or spent brass drills. For either, have someone load your revolver and not fill every cylinder with a live bullet, or mix live and spent rounds (just the empty cartridge) together, which helps so you can see any empty chambers during the drill. The key is to aim, pull, and control your fire the same way on every round, whether it's live or not. You know you've failed the empty cylinder drill when you jerk the trigger as it falls on to a dead hole.)

Strong trigger pull in double action, so make sure to practice in both single and double action. That said, it is not a good safety habit (and we've never seen any trained operator do it) to carry your revolver in single-action mode, with the hammer cocked back. You'll notice when you cock the hammer and put the gun into single-action mode, the trigger moves back, thereby changing the trigger pull (fairly dramatically) from five pounds to 1.5.

In General:

Revolvers can be good distance guns, but only if you practice. There are wizards out there who can hit bullseyes with a short-barreled two-inch revolver at 25, 50, and even 100 yards. Most normal people have to practice constantly to get and, more importantly, maintain that level of accuracy. Bes to use the snubnose for close-up shooting situations and practice accordingly.

It pays to start and stick to good tactical reloading habits with your revolver. This means you'll need to get comfortable using speedloaders. Just like when you change your magazines with your pistol, you must teach yourself to keep your eyes on the target as you do so. Stop looking at any gun when you reload. Look where the bad guy is or where he is moving to. You should already know how to make magazine or speedloader changes by feel, especially so you can make the ammo additions in low-light conditions.

Speedloaders work best when you let gravity help you, so once you dump your empty brass on to the ground, flip the revolver back and drop the new rounds from the speedloader downward, not sideways.

(Never dump your empty revolver brass into your hand for more than just a split-second before you let it drop the ground. Google the Newhall California Highway Patrol murders from 1971 for the reasons why we never put our empty brass or speedloaders into our pockets. Always dump your brass, speedloaders, and magazines on the ground whenever you practice at an outdoor range.)

No need to be a semi-auto snob. Save some room in your gun collection for a small-frame revolver and learn to love what it can do for you too.

CHAPTER 21

BRINGING YOUR GUN TO WORK

Here begins an interesting and challenging discussion about whether you can and should bring your weapon into your workplace. As we continue to watch in horror the targeting of gun-free zones, the debate over where you can legally carry concealed weapons is like watching a ping-pong match as the ball is slammed from side to side. The politicization of where, when, and why to carry (or even own guns) is served up after every event of workplace, school, or mass violence and all that misses the point of the importance and benefits of reasonable Concealed Carry.

Many workplaces do not have security guards, and many larger organizations that do have security as a function, contract for unarmed officers. Threats to the workplace, shopping centers, churches, sporting events, and any place where people gather in mass are not going away. The targeting of people has increased to include vehicle attacks on walkways, streets, and gathering places. The absence of security officers or having unarmed security does little to discourage thugs and cowards seeking a body count. If an organization or retail business is unable to stop or mitigate targeted violence, a person determined not to become a victim of violence may be compelled to protect themselves. Once an attack is initiated the likelihood of surviving without fighting back, while waiting for law enforcement to arrive, is low. It's not the fault of the police but the reality of the mass attack dynamics.

A sign on the parking lot entrance or in the window of a business proclaiming it a "Gun-Free Zone" appears to only apply to the law-abiding citizen and not the thug or coward. We can't imagine a nefarious actor seeking to harm his ex-wife or girlfriend at the only place he knows she will be every day to abide by the sign on the front window where she works. Can you?

What about the recently-fired employee unable to get another job, deciding to "teach his former boss a lesson" by shooting him and the HR Director in the reception area of his former facility? Do any of us believe for a moment that he will stop at the parking lot entrance or the lobby door because of the "No Weapons" posting?

What about a woman who has just taken out a Temporary Restraining Order (TRO) against her abusive boyfriend? She has tried every effort to protect herself, including notifying her employer, working with the police, and taking self-defense classes. While making every attempt to create a normal life for herself, she lives in fear that her abusive ex will find her and kill her. Does she have the right to use her legally-acquired firearm to protect herself should he arrive at her workplace? The answer is "not usually."

The gaps in reasonable means to provide and maintain a level of self-protection in an environment where threateners are encouraging the targeting of gun-free zones or areas where people are gathered in numbers, requires a serious consideration of how the legally-armed citizen can save themselves or others.

In our not-so-recent past, armed employees were expected to leave their guns in their vehicles in the company parking lot or locked up at home. This practice did not go unnoticed by nefarious actors, nor did it discourage them from attacking gun-free sites.

Current debates suggest the armed citizen is less likely to be victimized. Armed people at the worksite are also less likely to be victimized. We are finally seeing some schools deciding to arm certain qualified staff members, who volunteer to do it. We know armed security is a stronger deterrent than unarmed security, that's why professional executive bodyguards and Secret Service agents carry guns and not "Don't Shoot!" signs. Regardless of what anti-gun people want to believe, armed protection details are simply more protective than unarmed protection details. An interesting observation is that some of the loudest public voices against firearms are being protected by armed protection details. This irony escapes them.

With all this said, if your workplace establishes by policy that your facility is a gun-free zone, you are bound by the consequences of breaking that rule. (In other words, don't put your job at risk or get fired because of us.) We would hope you have the ability to calmly discuss with your company or agency leaders about the necessary protection protocols for preventing targeted violence that include active shooter responses similar to the national standard "Run-Hide-Fight" model.

If your workplace does not have a workplace violence

prevention policy (and many still don't), then we recommend you try to hold a polite and careful meeting to discuss their ability to provide site and personnel protection for everyone. Recent church shootings have many houses of worship re-looking at their policies and plans to provide trained and armed protection for their congregations.

Mike recently helped a local church discuss options to include allowing certain members to Carry Concealed with the proper training beyond the normal basic Concealed Carry classes. This follows a growing trend across the U.S., where citizens have decided enough is enough and being armed is a reasonable approach to enhance self and site protection. The demand for new gun purchases, Concealed Carry permits, and range training has increased exponentially as a direct result of the mass attacks we have all seen.

We can no more tell you to carry your gun at your place of work than we can tell you what weapon, holster, and type of ammunition to carry. What we can suggest is what we discussed in our chapter on practicing the 3 A's (Awareness, Avoidance, Action) approach is critical. Be aware that gun-free zones not only can be attacked but are more likely to. In your workplace, this might be caused by a disgruntled current or former employee, non-employees, or domestic violence spillovers from outside the workplace.

Be aware of what could happen at your workplace. Avoid people, situations, or places at your worksite where violence may develop or occur. Have an action plan for when you are unable to avoid trouble. Adopt the Department of Homeland Security's Run-Hide-Fight protocol if an active shooter event happens at your workplace. (Watch the video on YouTube; a partnership between the DHS and the City of Houston, Texas.)

There is no doubt that there are some employees who weigh the policy violation, need for security, and potential consequences and decide to Carry Concealed at work. There are many who have quoted the old adage: “I’d rather be judged by twelve than carried by six.” The growing support for the armed employee (especially on school campuses) to help in the overall protection posture has created a debate around Concealed Carry training. What this should mean is increased training in situational scenarios and frequent qualifications for those asked to use their Concealed Carry permits to help in site security. This won’t work if Concealed Carry permit holders have not shot, qualified (achieved a range score), or practiced. In the discussion about carrying concealed at work, we should enforce proper situational training associated with that workplace in addition to realistic situational scenarios supporting the whole life approach to carrying.

Practicing your “what ifs” when bringing your gun to work helps you to be prepared for possible life-threatening events or situations. It’s not going to be a simple adjustment to consider, develop, and practice situations to establish a mental and physical readiness without planning for them. In considering scenario events, what is the evacuation or response plan if there was an active shooter event at your worksite, with police responding? There is always the chance that a legally-armed employee will come face-to-face with the responding police team. Should the armed employee lock himself or herself down, or run towards the gunfire? Just because the employee is armed, is he or she expected to act as a security officer? Do you have the role and responsibility to stand in harm’s way?

An employee who is permitted to Carry Concealed is ideally expected to avoid a gunfight. Practicing his or her awareness and avoidance he or she is expected to watch and listen for an event that might be developing. The question becomes should he or she avoid contact with an active shooter or should he or she confront the shooter? The employee should make every attempt to avoid the action sequence of the 3 A's, but if all else fails, use his or her weapon to protect himself or herself and others. This choice of action during a gun battle may not be an easy decision or may cause delays in action. Part of being prepared is thinking, developing scenarios and practicing those hard-decision scenarios. Being a legally-armed employee in a stressful threat situation will no doubt be rough, but with frequent scenario-based training situations, your chance of survival is stronger.

Consider a scenario taking place in a real estate office with about thirty employees, located in a strip mall. Sandy, a 10-year real estate agent, now has her own office and also has a Concealed Carry permit and she diligently carries her Glock 43. Having her Concealed Carry has provided her with a stronger sense of security while showing properties and working alone in homes for sale. The office is abuzz with activity with an office party to begin shortly to celebrate a great year of sales. As Sandy sits at her desk, she hears yelling from the front reception area, which is about 20 yards and several offices over from her. At this point, Sandy is aware that something out of the norm is developing. Sandy moves toward her door to look towards the yelling. As she reaches her door, the sound of pops followed by immediate screaming erupts. Without hesitation, Sandy closes her door, pushes a chair against the door, and runs to her desk, grabbing her purse. The shots and screams become louder as the apparent shooter has moved past the reception area and through the office. Sandy grabs her Glock 43 and her spare mag and gets on the floor behind her desk, positioned out of direct sight with her weapon and points it at her closed door. The shooting continues with yelling by the shooter saying some usual version of "All are going to die today!"

Frightened, Sandy steadies her aim at the door, controls her breathing as practiced during her shooting scenarios, and waits as the shooter gets closer. The shooter attempts to open Sandy's door but it jams against the office chair she used as her best possible quick barricade. The shooter kicks the door open and enters, looking straight ahead, expecting to see Sandy standing or cowering in the corner. Sandy sees the shooter entering the room and, acting instead of reacting, she fires into the shooter's chest, emptying her magazine. The shooter is caught unaware and staggers from multiple jacketed hollow points exploding in his heart. His attack is over and Sandy reloads as the shooter takes a few steps back into the hallway and collapses. Sandy keeps her aim at the shooter just as she has trained.

As she stands, the sound of police sirens and employees' screaming jumbles into the echo in her head as she realizes she has just survived a workplace attack. Sandy places her handgun on her desk, raising her hands as the police move down the hall toward the shooter.

Sandy, like many Concealed Carriers, practiced Awareness, Avoidance, and Action skill-training. Sandy frequently trains and practices with her weapon. She was mentally prepared and trained for the eventuality of this moment and as a result, survived by keeping herself cool under duress. Sandy made every attempt to avoid the attack but when all else failed took a practiced approach and acted versus reacting. She survived.

CHAPTER 22

RETAIL STORE ROBBERIES

If you own a retail store of any type where you see live customers inside your premises, you're a potential robbery target. Robbers don't really care what you sell – donuts, jewelry, burgers, antiques, frozen yogurt, gas, office supplies, clothes, if you have cash on the premises – and there doesn't even have to be that much of it on hand – they will try to rob you for it.

Despite the presence of cameras, time-controlled safes, and even armed and unarmed security officers, the number of convenience store, gas station, and retail store robberies continues to rise from year to year.

According to the FBI's annual Uniform Crime Report for 2016, "The average dollar value of property stolen per reported robbery was $1,400. Robberies accounted for an estimated $465 million in losses. Banks experienced the highest average dollar loss at $3,531 per offense. Compared with 2015, the report found that the number of robberies at convenience stores rose the most among six of the seven locations tracked in 2016. Last year there were 17,401 robberies of convenience stores, a 6.7% increase from 2015. For gas and service stations, there were 8,178 robberies, up 2.1% from 2015." (www.UCR.FBI.gov)

Way, way back in 1996, the Athena Research Corporation conducted a study using interviews with incarcerated c-store robbers. Not surprisingly, the research was funded by The Southland Corporation, the franchiser for the 7-11 chain of convenience stores. Can we still learn the lessons from this report over three decades ago to still be applicable today? Of course.

- The researchers interviewed 181 armed robbers in five state prisons in New Jersey, Texas, Illinois, California, and Louisiana.

- The study indicates that for the majority of robbers, their ***first*** priority was to target stores near easy escape routes. Their ***second*** priority was to pick a store with easy access to cash. As one inmate put it, what ***kept*** him from robbing a store was "a bad escape route and a cashier who [safe] drops the cash too often."

- The majority of robbers said that alarms, cameras and the threat of long sentences didn't deter them, although these devices and punishments make it easier for us to catch them and lock them up later.

- The proximity of the store played an interesting part in their choices. (Perhaps these guys were geography enthusiasts in school.) From a "Here's how we can catch them" perspective, one fact emerges in red and blue flashing lights: Over 40 %

of the robbers ***lived less than two miles*** from the convenience store they chose to hit.

- With this in mind, the police must continue to focus their patrol activities to look for cars or suspects matching the descriptions within a few minutes driving distance of the target store.

- In terms of multiple offenses, over one-third of the crooks had committed at least five or more convenience store robberies. The average number, before being caught, was 13. This should reaffirm our belief that c-store robberies are crimes for the recidivist, serial, or repeat robber, the one who chooses these places as their "crime of choice," over street muggings or bank robberies.

- The study raises a serious police and employee safety issue as well. Over ***60%*** of the robbers said they robbed the stores with a partner. \This accomplice worked either as a getaway driver/armed lookout in the parking lot or as an in-store armed lookout.

- Most store clerks focus only upon the man pointing the big gun at them, and thus, can give only one suspect description. This should give you more to think about if you are confronted by an armed robber inside or near a convenience store; chances are good that he has at least one other player in his crew.

- Whether it was crook bravado or the truth, the majority of the robbers said that the number of people inside the store - employees, witnesses - made no difference to them in terms of deterring their robberies. Most thought that with "a gun and a partner, they could take on/takedown about 11 people."

- The number or gender of the clerks or the presence of an unarmed security guard did little to deter these crooks. But while they admitted that they were more deterred by an armed security guard or the possibility of an armed clerk, they felt their chances of survival or escape were still good, since they believed their opponents would not shoot or be able to hit them during the crime.

- While "easy" cash was a requirement for the robbers, the amount they needed was not huge. Most described their need for money as "at least $200." In other words, they both expected to get this much and they would be willing to rob the store if they thought they could get this much money. The study authors attribute this small cash amount to the cheap price and easy availability of street drugs. That is, crooks would take the risk of arrest or getting shot since the payoff provided at least enough money (however briefly) for drugs.

- Most c-store policies instruct their employees not to resist the robber in any way. Other research reports have agreed by concluding that store clerks who resisted were almost 50 times more likely to be killed than those who "cooperated, gave up the money, did not make any sudden moves, did not talk, stare [for better suspect descriptions], or try to be a hero."

- This study concurs with this, as the robbers agreed that "most people get hurt when they resist, keep their hands out of sight, or make sudden moves." The other reason for injuries was because the robber was "nervous or high on drugs."

- Criminologists talk about the crime fantasies or "scripts" crooks run through their heads in the days or weeks before they commit their crimes. Robbers often say the same things during the robbery because that's how they've practiced it over and over. Store employees can get hurt or shot when they "interrupt" these scripts by failing to follow the instructions or moving in a way that deviates from the crook's original plan.

- It's surprising to learn that so few of the c-store robbers cared about the presence of video surveillance cameras. They rationalized this belief by stating that "no one is watching the monitor at the time of the robbery" and that "they could always wear a disguise" if they thought cameras were in operation.

- Further, the robbers heartily agreed that robbery is a tough crime to solve and they rarely gave much thought to being caught or locked up for a long period of time.

- And the presence of police in the neighborhoods around the convenience store did little to stop these men. They believed that the police could not always be near these stores because of other service calls and some admitted to planning their crimes around police shift changes.

This study summarizes some useful conclusions as to how to prevent convenience store robberies: keep the amount of available cash in the drawers down to an absolute minimum; put more barriers in the store to make it hard for the crook to get in and out quickly (displays, aisles, counters, turnstiles, double doors); install fences or gates to block off the rear of the store (a favorite pre-robbery hiding place or post-robbery escape route); install speed bumps and concrete planter boxes in parts of the parking lot to make it tougher on the getaway driver; and continue to use high-quality video camera systems to help the police get a good look at the crooks when they case or rob the stores.

And as for the robbers' claims that they can wear masks and similar disguises to avoid being recognized on tape, we know many of them favor the same shirt, jacket, hat, and sunglasses in each robbery. They get their media or police nicknames, i.e. "the Red Ski Mask Bandit" or "the Oakland Raiders Jacket Robber" from their idiotic desire to wear their "lucky" clothes time after time.

Since the employee turnover rate for gas stations, liquor, and convenience stores tends to be quite high, owners and managers can find themselves in a near-constant training, reminding, and security awareness-building mode with new employees.

For your retail store, consider the following employee training reminders to reduce the likelihood and impact of a robbery:

- One robber at the counter usually means one or more inside or outside the store too. Remind all employees to look for who the robber came in with or left with.

- Train your employees to call 911 first, and speak to the police immediately as soon as it is safe. When they first call their parents, loved ones, or the store manager, it significantly delays the police response time and their ability to catch the robber(s).

- Create a pre-printed checklist for employees to write down the description of the suspect (or suspects and any related vehicles) after he has fled.

- Don't reveal too much about your security equipment or procedures to every employee. All store security information (safe combinations, alarms codes, location of the floor safe, camera or DVR access, etc.,) should be given out on a "need to know" basis.

- Warn your employees not to have any discussions about cash amounts or security devices or procedures, on or off the job, even with family members.

- Create a fake set of keys and a staged "throw down" wallet filled with a few one-dollar bills to keep at the register, in case the robber asks for the employee's actual car keys and wallet. Train the employees to give up these decoys instead.

- Develop special security procedures for when lone employees have to leave the floor, or go on restroom breaks, garbage runs, or freezer work.

- Install a high-quality camera and a large TV monitor at the main entrance to your store, to let everyone see themselves big and bold, as they enter.

- Make the investment in digital CCTV cameras, with accompanying DVR hard drives or network software; they will pay for themselves over time.

- Encourage your employees to pay closer attention to potential robbers the moment they enter the store. Casers often come in a few hours before the robbery, most often on the same day, to make sure nothing has changed from the last time. Since robbers often wear the same clothes (plus a hat or a mask), the police will often want to review the video footage going back several hours.

- Keep the back door of the store, restaurant, and business, locked at all times. If you need ventilation, put up a steel door.

- Keep the merchandise and advertising signs out of the street-sight lines, so they don't block the window views from the outside looking in or vice-versa, for customers or passing police cars.

- Although stores certainly get robbed during daylight hours, teach your employees to have "Sundown Vigilance" and increase their security awareness after dusk.

- Take better care of your money. Be more security-conscious while handling it in bulk. If you have to help the employee with change, close the register temporarily (or even close the store briefly), and do it discreetly or in another room with a locked door.

- Change the daily routine for depositing the cash. Use different people, times, cars, methods, bags, and routes to the bank. Or consider investing in an armored car service as a group or in your strip mall.

- Many robbers case the store one to four hours before the incident, often wearing the same clothing, minus their hats or masks. Don't be afraid to look directly at store or car casers. Let them know they have been seen.

- Call your local station and ask the officers/deputies who work the area to introduce themselves. (Cops frequent stores with safe bathrooms, good coffee [not free], friendly clerks, and where they don't have to "work" on their breaks.)

- Remove all posters from the windows, create a full line of sight, keep the rear doors locked, and maintain the interior and exterior lighting fixtures.

- Discuss your response to a "simulated weapon" robbery. Is it a drunk or an addict? Teenager? Mentally ill? Hardcore crook? Not every robbery situation should require the employee to just hand over the money. We don't want them to be a hero, but common sense says you don't give a penny to a naked man who comes in with a demand note.

- When working alone with a person in the store, use a "phantom employee callout" to make it seem like more than one is on duty. This could sound like, "I'll take care of the customer Jerry, and you just keep working back there."

- Watch for "distraction teams" – a screaming woman, a crying baby, or an injured person. Keep your eyes on seemingly unrelated people wanting to grab the register and run out with it.

- Keep all store and register keys separate from house or car keys.

- Be extra vigilant during opening or closing times, employee shift changes, and police shift changes.

- No sudden moves during an actual robbery. Talk quietly, try not to look directly at the crook for too long, and don't ask questions.

- Open the register and step back from the counter s-l-o-w-l-y. Consider turning sideways from the robber to blade yourself and make for less of a center-mass target.

- Keep your hands low, not raised up or hidden.

- Don't stare or argue.

- Always believe there are at least two robbers. One robber at the counter might mean one or more inside or outside the store or restaurant as well.

- Keep the windows and the store aisles clear for better visibility.

- Don't reveal every security procedure to all your employees. Keep some policies or knowledge about security equipment to yourself.

- Never talk about how much money your business is making, especially to the media.

- Make the investment in a digital camera system you can access from your laptop or from home.

- Make sure whatever camera system you choose is installed correctly. The image must be visible at night and in bright sunlight. Test the camera views regularly.

- Use a digital camera system where the images are stored on to the DVR hard drive and be copied to a CD later for the police.

- Camera systems don't just act as a deterrent to help with robbery prevention or investigations; they can prevent false slip and fall cases or monitor employee theft.

- Never install fake cameras. Having a camera system that does not record or displays only to a TV screen is useless and may cause liability for you.

- Armed security guards are not a good replacement for cameras; they're mutually exclusive.

- Change the position of the security guards frequently. Sometimes their visual presence is useful, other times they should watch from a position of stealth inside or outside the store.

- Install speed bumps in the parking lot, especially if you're freeway-close.

- Casers usually come in two to three hours before the robbery, most often on the same day, to make sure nothing has changed from the last time they cased it. Jewelry store casers may make many trips to the site.

- Do the best you can to discourage your employees from talking to anyone about money or security procedures. Many robberies are inside jobs, either by the employees, friends of the employees, of friends of friends of the employees. Some robbers are good social engineers and may even talk to employees about security procedures or devices in seemingly casual conversations.

- The more robberies the suspect has done in the past, the braver he may feel. This can be good or bad, since he may be less frightened and therefore more aggressive, or more in control and less likely to screw it up and shoot someone.

- After a robbery, train all employees to quickly lock the store and call the police.

- Train your employees on how to protect the crime scene for the police, by touching nothing the robber touched.

- Crooks want freeway closeness, exits near freeways; they don't want to drive aimlessly or rapidly through unfamiliar streets.

- The motive for nearly all robberies is to support a drug habit, a gambling habit, or both. A small number of robberies are done by new or wannabe gang members, usually told to by a shot caller, and in the company of a hardcore gangster. These young people can be dangerous.

- Create a preprinted checklist for the employee to write down the description of the suspect after he has fled.

- Use the services of the D.A.'s Office Victim-Witness program.

- If you choose to protect yourself with your gun, shoot at what you're aiming at, knowing you are fully responsible for every round. Know your background and don't miss the bad guy and hit a customer inside or even outside the store. Know that you don't have to "fight fair" by telling the crook to "Drop the gun!" If you're threatened by an armed attacker, end the fight before he can do the same to you. He knew the risk of being killed by you or the cops when he entered the store with the intent to commit and armed robbery.

If you own a retail store and hold a Concealed Carry permit, this study tells us some new information and reminds us that what we already know about convenience store robbers: they are dangerous and here to stay.

CHAPTER 23

GIVE UP YOUR MONEY OR YOUR LIFE? NO TO EITHER

If you own a retail store of any type, the usual advice from the police (and probably your business insurance company) is to hand over the cash from the register or the safe if you are ever confronted by an armed robber. And you get this same advice, as all bank tellers know, to give up the money even if they don't show an obvious weapon or just use a demand note. It's not bad advice for your employees; you don't want them to get injured or killed protecting your money. That's why you have insurance. You can replace the money but you can't bring them back from the dead.

The police give the same advice about your money and possessions during a street mugging or a carjacking: "Your cash or your car is not worth your life. Let the robber have it."

Robbers and other crooks with guns must see or hear these same Public Service Announcements because they always expect people to give up when they show their weapons or point them at them.

I prefer the "Samuel L. Jackson as Jules Winnfield" approach. If you recall the scene in Quentin Tarantino's masterful 1994 film "Pulp Fiction," a male and female robber get the drop on Jackson in an LA diner. The male robber – played by Tim Roth and known as "Pumpkin" until Jackson starts calling him "Ringo" for his British accent – points his gun at Jackson as he sits in the booth eating his breakfast. Jackson says to Ringo, "I hate to shatter your ego but this ain't the first time I've had a gun pointed at me."

While this may not be true for everyone reading this, Steve only had a gun pointed at him – drilled into the back of his head, to be specific – one time, and that was enough. When Steve was 15 and working at a small grocery store, his partner and he got robbed by two guys with guns who came in at closing time. After they ran off with $888 (a lot of money in 1978), at some point that night Steve thought, "This is bullshit. This will never happen to me again. No one will ever, ever get the tactical advantage on me again. I'm going to become a cop." Which he did and no one ever pointed a gun at him again, lucky for him, so he didn't get shot or have to kill that person.

Back to the movie: Ringo tries to make Jules give up his boss's briefcase, by threatening to shoot him in the face. He does not see Jackson is pointing his own gun at him under the table. Jules swiftly turns the tables on Ringo and soon he is pressing the barrel of his 9mm against Ringo's neck. It's a tense scene that ends in a mostly satisfying way for all concerned.

Point: Just because the bad guy has a gun doesn't mean you

are overwhelmed, out of the fight, or about to be shot. (Some crooks carry unloaded guns for their own reasons.) Even if you do get shot that doesn't mean you will die. Turn the tables! Fight back! Be aggressively offensive and not passively defensive.

Another scene from another favorite movie, the 1941 classic, "The Maltese Falcon." In an early part of the film, Joel Cairo (played so perfectly by Peter Lorre) meets private eye Sam Spade (Humphrey Bogart) in Spade's office and tries to figure out if he has the black bird statue the whole movie is about. Cairo pulls a gun on Spade, who disarms him and knocks him out.

Coming to, Cairo says, "I am prepared to pay five thousand for the figure's return. You have it?"

Spade says, "No."

Cairo says, "If it is not here, why should you have risked serious injury to prevent my searching for it?"

Spade says, "I should sit around and let people come in and stick me up?"

In other words, I'm not going to be held at gunpoint by the likes of you.

There is brave and there is stupid and perhaps, there is stupidly brave. Call it what you want. Crooks expect compliance from sheep. Bullies expect scared students, co-workers, or their employees to back down and go along with their bullying. Robbers expect people to give up their cars, wallets, purses, and cell phones without a fight.

We say your motto should be: "Not Me, Not Ever. I will

Never Give Up My Safety or the Safety of My Family Without Fighting Back."

Our families already know this. Should we ever get mugged, carjacked, or otherwise assaulted by one or more thugs, that someone or a mouth-breather in that group is going to get shot, by us, during the expected time of compliance.

We are not speaking foolishly, just honestly. We will not give up or give in. We will go for our guns and count on our experience, training, and guts to beat you to the trigger, bad guy. And even if we get shot, that doesn't mean we are out of the fight.

You should say this out loud from time to time and believe it always:

"Attention Bad Guys: You will not catch me off guard at the ATM; the mall parking lot after the movies have ended; at the restaurant; at the grocery store; or in my car. I will have seen you coming long before and made ready for you. I will not give up anything you want and I will beat you because you are not expecting me to fight back. You think I will act like the other people you have victimized. (And there are probably dozens of people you have frightened or injured before you ever get or got caught.) Imagine the look of surprise on your face when I shoot you without "fair warning" because I don't do or say what people on TV do or say. Threaten me and I will not fight fair because there is no such thing.

"If you are stupid enough to come close enough to me with your gun and I cannot get to mine in time, I will disarm you. This will happen because you cannot react as fast as I can act and by the time you decide to pull the trigger, I will have redirected your gun barrel away from me, closed my hand over your slide or cylinder, bladed myself in case you do get a shot off, and bent your finger back until it snaps. I will take your gun away and draw my own.

"Any further attacks on your part will result in me putting one or more carefully-placed bullets into you. Best to give up son, assume the same prone position you did after your last police chase or as you learned in the prison yard, and wait safely for the arrival of the cops. I will make sure you are not harmed as you rest and sweat facedown on the pavement. Sorry, but you picked the wrong guy."

CHAPTER 24

MIKE'S READY KIT AND GO BAG ESSENTIALS

You never know you're missing something until you really need it. And it's never more alarming or frustrating than when that need is during a crisis.

As a goal, I always seek to find the best path in a situation, but prepare and train for the worst. Maintaining my "Ready Kit" and "Go Bag" assures me I have what I need when I need it. What my Ready Kit and Go Bag look like may vary depending upon my travel area and my activities. A one-solution set-up is not necessarily the answer, so what follows are some thoughts about what you might need for Every Day Carry (EDC) and Go Bags.

"Ever vigilant" is a lifestyle cornerstone of maintaining readiness, which means always, always, and always assess your surroundings and situation with the gear you may need to use.

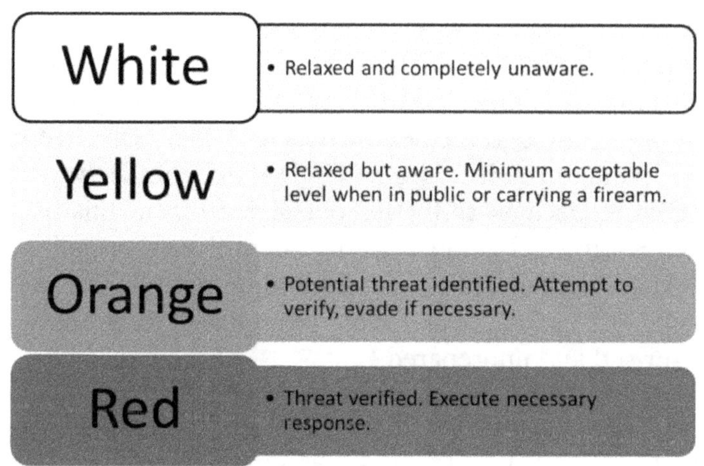

USMC Colonel Jeff Cooper's Color Codes

The Color Codes for Danger was developed by USMC Col. Jeff Cooper, the founder of the Gunsite Academy.

In your Concealed Carry lifestyle, Condition "White" is a zone we should never allow ourselves to stay in, unless you're in a well-protected location. At a minimum, "Yellow" is our comfort zone and essential to "ever vigilant" readiness. "Orange" means you have to read to the situation and get out or prepare to defend yourself. "Red" means it's time to fight. Through training and preparation, moving from Yellow to Orange to Red and back again can become smoother and less hectic, and, if you are properly geared, can assure greater chances of success.

USAF Colonel John Boyd's "OODA Loop" was the foundational approach to getting inside the threat curve of your enemy in battle. "Observe, orient, decide, and act" was the basis to his becoming an ace fighter pilot. For years, OODA was the ideal way to find the winning path.

Recent changes in aggressor tactics and the needed

readiness essential to survive have prompted a change from OODA to ROAPA. Many years ago, Steve and I were teaching a Contact and Cover class in Pennsylvania to a group of law enforcement officers. In that class, we started the paradigm shift from OODA to our newly-created ROAPA, because of the lessons learned from Jihadist terror tactics towards law enforcement. By targeting law enforcement and citizens, too often they were catching them off guard, and when the attack came they were surprised and unprepared.

ROAPA stands for: **Recognize, Orientate, Assess, Position,** and **Act.** For law enforcement officers making a car stop or responding to a call, it's essential to "recognize" that the bad actor or a threat has the command and control of the area or environment the officer is approaching.

"Recognize" means we may not have command and that we could be in an area or attack sequence designed and set up by the bad guy.

"Orientate" means we carefully and purposely orientate ourselves to the zone and environment we are responding to. If the officer is approaching a car, or if the officer Lights up" a car and the driver suddenly pulls into an alley, the real question is, who selected that spot for the car to stop? The officer or the possible bad guy? By orientating yourself to the surroundings, you recognize the alley, buildings left and right near the car, and maybe even a set of trash dumpsters that could be hiding a threat.

"Assess" means you quickly scan the rooftops, entry doors, and dark areas, considering a threat could be in any of these places, and the area where the car stopped could be part of an ambush plan. Ambushes by throwing bricks from building tops, pre-planned explosives, and attacks by pre-staged persons must be factored in when you are drawn into an area not of your choosing.

“Position” means you select your approach and positioning considering the potential for attack.

“Act” means you were ready for this situation, trained and prepared, avoided any surprises, and acted with decisiveness when called upon.

Your Ready Kit and Go Bag needs to match the environment, area, or zone that you are in or will be entering. At your house, you should have a Ready Kit and a Go Bag. In the car, you should have a Ready Kit and a Go Bag. Out and about, you might be suited up with either a Ready Kit or a Go Bag with you, in a backpack or a briefcase. At work, you might have a Ready Kit with you and a Go Bag in the car (or your locked desk drawer or securable work area).

I am a frequent traveler and when RON (remaining overnight) in a hotel, I have a Ready Kit and a Go Bag.

My Ready Kit is the old fanny pack-style Concealed Carry bag with my primary firearm, two spare mags, a flashlight and spare batteries, two ChemLights, a CAT tourniquet, and a folding knife.

In my Go Bag, which is my tactical backpack, I have: a ballistic panel, my full-frame semi-auto pistol, spare IWB and OWB holsters, four spare mags (these mags can fit into the smaller primary carry), folding and fixed blade knives, a flashlight, batteries, my EDC first-aid kit, ChemLights, my wallet, personal items needed for fast exits, charging gear for phones or tablets, any maps, a few energy bars, some water, minimal clothes, a light outer jacket or shirt (weather depending), a pair of gloves, and my Gerber multi-tool.

My home kit is much different, as I live in a more rural setting and need a way to have the proper gear at hand. My home kit is either a vest or a ready-belt with my firearm, holster, spare mags for pistol and carbine, flashlight, knife, CAT tourniquet, my Gerber multi-tool, ChemLights, and a night vision monocular.

Both my carbine and pistol have mounted lights. Living in a rural setting, the outside world can present you with some challenges, such as wild dogs, coyotes, snakes, or unwanted human visitors. At home, your house itself can be your kit, with properly distributed gear in strategic areas. These locations require careful consideration in order to prevent children and others from ever getting access to your weapons.

I'll admit that Ready Kits and Go Bags may be a bridge too far for many. My gear choices and readiness ideas are born from situations where I or others working with or for me didn't have certain necessary gear, either because they or I forgot it or they didn't think it was necessary.

It's interesting that many people who Carry Concealed spend lots of selection time and money on their gun, ammunition, sights, and holsters, but don't see the bigger picture in being prepared with additional gear. Some just head to the range, not having the gear they carry or plan to use in the street.

How do you determine what is enough gear or training? Have you been in a situation where you didn't have the right backup gear? Can you grab your Ready Kit and have what you need to leave your house in mere minutes, when faced with a threatening event? Do you have a Ready Kit and Go Bag in your vehicle that will make you feel secure if you are traveling across the country and break down? Do you feel ready while staying overnight in a hotel to be able to exit in an emergency and be ready to face a threatening situation? If you plan to Carry Concealed, do you feel ready to have what you need when you need it? What's in your Ready Kit and Go Bag and why?

CHAPTER 25

MIKE'S UNUSUAL RANGE BAG AND GEAR ESSENTIALS

Some may say my range **bag** is really my range **truck**, as I have collected an over-abundance of firearms and self-protection-related items for my own training and to train others. Having a key to our outside multi-hundred-acre range provides me the luxury to carry in my gear, set up my own firing bay, and shoot, shoot, shoot.

My gear collection has grown over the years as I adjusted my needs from changing weapons, optics, carry methods, and tactics. Some items I intuitively knew would be "must haves" and others I acquired through "oh crap, the batteries died" situations, or when I needed a new tool or two.

Here is a list of the key range gear you should consider as essential to helping you create a great training day:

1. Eye protection
2. Hearing protection

3. Hat
4. Range first-aid kit (which should include at least one combat-level tourniquet)
5. Carry and training ammunition
6. Carry and training weapons
7. Spare magazines in all sizes, to match your weapons
8. Magazine loading gear or devices (to save your fingers)
9. Targets
10. Target tape to cover previous bullet holes
11. Felt marking pen
12. Black spray paint
13. Target stands
14. Target posts
15. IDPA cardboard targets
16. Spotting scope
17. Binoculars
18. Flashlight
19. Spare batteries for any device that needs a battery
20. Tools for weapons, scope tuning
21. Staple gun
22. Duct tape
23. Plastic tie wraps
24. Cell phone
25. Hand wipes/cleaner
26. Glass lens cleaners
27. Spare holsters and magazine holders
28. Pen and paper
29. Concealed Carry training jacket or shirt
30. Small cut or abrasion bandages
31. Weapon field cleaning kit
32. Range/distance finder
33. Training timer

Some of our more unusual gear includes:

1. Dummy rounds for failure drills
2. Red gun for walkthroughs
3. Shooting chronograph
4. Weapon rests/mounts/sand bags
5. Shooting sticks
6. Weather/wind meter
7. Bore sights
8. Shooting stools or chairs

As you can see, it's much more than just "gear in a gear bag" for me.

Each range membership and range access you go to will have a set of rules and regulations for safety training. Be sure to follow their safety rules to the letter.

A short list of gear for an indoor range session might include:

1. Weapon and holster
2. Training ammunition
3. Gun case
4. Spare magazines
5. Magazine loader/unloader
6. First-aid kit
7. A gun cleaning kit

What every outdoor or indoor range visit should include is a **training mindset**. What's my goal for this training session? What do I need to work on and how can I better myself in the time that I have?
Besides the goal-orientated thoughts, we must be aware of our range surroundings, including the weather for outdoor range use and any safety hazards.

It's worth repeating that the Concealed Carry lifestyle begins and ends with your mindset. You should "train as you seek to perform; since you will perform as you have trained." What does this mean? In a crisis situation, you will likely react and revert back (or fall back) to what you already know. If you don't practice malfunction drills, or low light situations, or shooting around cover and concealment, you will probably not act appropriately in a truly stressful situation. If you don't practice reloading, how can you expect to reload under stress? If you don't practice other-hand, support hand, or off-hand shooting, you may not be able to draw your weapon and fire effectively. If you haven't repeatedly practiced other-hand, support hand, or off-hand draws, how can you expect to pull your weapon from concealment and save yourself under life-threatening stress?

On the other hand, if you visit the range with a plan, to work on skills you would likely experience during a street situation, you are less likely to freeze, act confused, or stare wide-eyed at the bad guy. This is why your mindset and training plan needs to be part of your range gear collection and training day preparation.

A large part of your daily mindset when armed is your ability to have a constant sense of vigilance-based "Awareness, Avoidance, and Action" thinking. Every one of your range visits should begin with being aware that you are in an environment where multiple visitors have deadly weapons around you and accidents could occur. Awareness involves the knowledge that some people visiting the range may not have the same required safety mindset. Awareness includes knowing that over the years, gun range have been places where accidental shootings, suicides, and homicides (the tragic murder of Chris Kyle being one of the best known) have occurred. There is never a time when I visit a range that I don't consider some negligent or nefarious activity as a possibility.

Avoidance means not ignoring your intuition that a situation or location is dangerous. If you feel that something, or someone, or a particular situation is unsafe, you should: not enter, leave, seek cover until it's safely resolved, and/or advise the onsite range officials. Muzzle discipline is not strictly practiced by all persons who visit a range, but your safety starts with you being aware and avoiding potential incidents, accidents, or hazards.

Range visits should be about more than your quarterly or

annual qualification shoots. Range days provide an opportunity to train with a purpose and specific goals, to develop the skills necessary to replace your panic-freeze reaction, and prepare to pre-act versus react. Range days allow you to build your range toolkit to match your goals.

A training mindset, matched with specific goals to improve, is the foundation for creating your range bag gear list. Having a plan allows you to gear up and match your Concealed Carry lifestyle. Train as you would everyday carry to include the right kinds of clothing, holsters, holster carry positions, holster draws, types of potential shooting situations, low light work, positions of cover, moving around corners, strong/off-support hand shooting, reloading, and reholstering.

Not having a lot of the necessary gear on the list above can pose challenges and potentially create an issue of your unpreparedness. And we know both lists and checklists are an important element of being organized and efficient (as any private or commercial pilot will tell you). However, over-relying on lists can remove your ability to think quickly and clearly and to align your response thoughts to a particular situation. Lists are only guidelines, to help you prepare your mindset for many situations. Mindset thinking provides some "bench strength" to develop what ifs and how tos to be prepared and not surprised.

I have a red dot reflex sight that's powered by a battery. Having the means to quickly and safely replace that battery, and having a secondary sighting capability is always a part of my mindset.

At my range, I'm lucky to have the ability to match my training with potential opportunities in my Concealed Carry daily life, like drawing and shooting from a vehicle, creating simulated street or combat situations, fixing malfunctions, and doing many kinds of off-hand drills.

Your preparation list should begin and end with a mindset that ensures you can match your necessary gear with your training regime. Range days provide you with an opportunity to practice and train in those situations you hope you never face, but if you do it will not be unfamiliar.

CHAPTER 26

INDOOR AND OUTDOOR RANGE SAFETY ISSUES

In our Perfect World, every range you shoot at, indoors or out, would have a qualified Rangemaster, who not only has gun safety, firearms-handling (pistol, revolver, rifle, shotgun), and gun malfunction-fixing skills, but knows gunshot-related first-aid and is already carrying or has immediate access to a kit that includes clotting bandages and a combat-level tourniquet. This person would be there to make sure none of the below happens on his or her watch:

Careless Muzzle Sweeps – "None of my guns have ever gone off when I wasn't actually pressing on the trigger." This may be true but would you bet your life on that conclusion? Should you allow someone (stupidly) pointing a gun at you to come to that same conclusion? Machines fail, and we're too often surprised when they do. Better to assume they will fail, malfunction, or even fire at will, and not be too shocked when it might just happen. People have dropped guns and they have fired. Model 1911-type guns in the Condition One "cocked and locked" category (hammer back, round chambered, thumb safety on, full magazine in place) have had discharges for whatever reason. Pointing a gun at any human or object you are not willing to destroy, however briefly, is the first step toward a tragedy.

Horseplay – This is rare at ranges with a skilled Rangemaster standing behind the line, but I've seen lots of unsafe screwing around when guys (and their beers) get together to shoot stuff in the desert, backwoods, or forest. Want proof of this? Just look at the amount of "Shooting Accident" videos (341,000 when I last looked) on YouTube. Alcohol, cellphone cameras, carelessness with guns to the extreme, and no range rules are a recipe for a bullet in the ass, or worse.

Not Wearing Ear and Eye Protection – "Eye protection is for pussies." This guy's tune changes when he is sitting in the Emergency Room, waiting for the ophthalmology surgeon to come and remove the metal fragments from his eye. Shooting without ear protection usually happens when people are messing around in a homemade or country range. One gun blast can permanently damage your hearing.

Some of the hazards from range practice come from the lead particles and gunpowder residue left on your hands. Always wash your hands with quality lead-cleaning soap before you leave the facility. The cumulative effects of lead are not good for your body.

Being Uneducated, Untrained, Stupid, or Ignorant About How Guns Work and About How Your Gun Works – We all know what happens when we assume things.

Trigger Finger Spasm – This is a real thing, especially under stress. We teach cops not to put their trigger finger inside the trigger guard until they are on target and ready to fire. They don't often listen and the results range from comical to fatally disastrous. Military personnel have much better trigger discipline and we should all learn from them.

Not Following a Precise Gun Malfunction Protocol – It's more than just Tap-Rack-Bang, or whatever variation of that you were taught. Malfunctions come in all shapes and sizes and you need to slow down your response to them, not speed it up. I get it that in a tactical situation, being fast is how you stay alive, even with a gun jam on your hands. But on the range, you need to follow a clearing protocol that has both major and minor steps to it, similar to this:

Stop all movements.
Look at your gun carefully.
Think about what you need to do before you do it (knowing there may be more than one solution to the current problem or more than one malfunction problem).
Correct the problem, safely, effectively, and quickly.
Stop all movements again, for a brief moment.
Look at your gun and what is going on around you, carefully.
Think about anything else you need to do before you fire.
Resume firing.

Male Macho Behavior or Showing Off – This is especially likely in front of a woman or a group of new gun owners. This includes screwing around with Bronco Billy quickdraws, or trick shots, or shooting at stuff which isn't meant to be shot at. Don't allow this from your buddies, ever. Your Rule of Thumb should always be: "I don't shoot with people who are not safe."

Fear of the Gun or the Shooting Experience – Loud bangs make most people flinch, including experienced shooters. Start by doubling up your hearing protection: put in foam earplugs and wear well-rated hearing protection. You'll still be able to hear your pals or the range people talking to you, but it can cut the noise level down and minimize your flinch.

New shooters are often fearful of their guns because they have not had enough formal training. Their mistakes are common: flinching from the noise made by their own gun and those guns around them; getting hit once by hot brass on the neck or face and overreacting to the burn; looking over the top of their gun to see where the round went (usually low or off target); not holding the pistol tightly enough, or so tightly their hands shake; and not knowing how to clear jams or malfunctions like soft strikes and double feeds.

Speed for No Good Reason – Fast out of the holster is great, unless you fire into the ground or your leg (or worse, your groin, which is the exact sound you'll make if a bullet heads there). Careful first, then fast, no matter what you're doing with the pistol. Slow everything down at the range: walking out to or changing your target, picking up your empty brass, reloading, changing guns or holsters, or moving from the rear bench to the firing line. Speed wins but it also kills. Be methodical in your movements. Besides driving a car, handling a gun is the easiest and fastest way to injure or kill yourself or others when you get complacent, skip safety steps, or develop bad habits.

Moving Toward Targets While Others Are Still Shooting – This happens at makeshift outdoor ranges, with no real (and trained) Rangemaster in charge. People walking toward their targets while others are still shooting sounds stupid and something you wouldn't ever do, but it seems to happen a lot when someone is not in charge of the line. Listen carefully to the commands on the line. Raise your non-gun hand if you have a question. Don't assume (see above) everyone is as safety-conscious as you.

Not Working In Enough Light – Some ranges are just movie theater dark. We're not always sure of their reasoning why, but some ranges illuminate the target area with a lot of light but the range line itself is dark. This can make your low-light training effective but working with or looking at your gun generally difficult. Choose a range lane with enough light.

Vanity – If you need them, wear your glasses so you can see what you're doing.

CHAPTER 27

THE HOMELAND SECURITY INVESTIGATIONS OFFICE SHOOTINGIN LONG BEACH, CA: SSA PERRY WOO'S STORY OF WORKPLACE VIOLENCE, TRAUMA, AND RECOVERY

What started out as a late afternoon meeting on February 16, 2012, at the Homeland Security Investigations (HSI), Long Beach, CA field office, with his supervisor and one of his employees, ended in gunfire, death, and heroism for HSI Assistant Special Agent in Charge Perry Woo. Deputy Special Agent in Charge (DSAC) Kevin Kozak, a 30-year veteran of Customs and HSI, was shot seven times in his office by HSI Supervisory Special Agent Ezekiel "Zeke" Garcia. Perry Woo shot Garcia as a last resort, during a workplace violence incident in Kozak's office in the Glenn M. Anderson Federal Building. In the end, Kozak survived his wounds, Garcia died at the scene, and Woo came away from the event knowing that his training and his will to survive made the difference in a tragic situation.

Supervisory Special Agent Woo has told his story of

survival, involving "blue on blue" workplace violence – where a law enforcement officer is the perpetrator – to many law enforcement groups around the country. He called it "a day I could have died." Woo, with 20 years of law enforcement experience both as a California police officer and special agent, previously received several commendations for his federal undercover work and his expertise in child exploitation crimes in Southeast Asia with the U.S. Customs Service, prior to this agency being consolidated into the U.S. Department of Homeland Security (DHS) after the 9/11 terrorist attacks.

At the time of the incident, Kevin Kozak was one of two DSACs in charge for the HSI, Los Angeles field office. Woo worked for Kozak for 6 years. SSA Zeke Garcia had worked for Kozak for 6 years and Woo for 6 months.

Garcia had worked for the U.S. Immigration & Naturalization Service since 1988 and this agency was also consolidated into DHS. Woo had been a fellow group supervisor with Garcia prior to his own promotion and both had a good working relationship. He had tried to help Garcia cope with several on and off-the-job stressors for several months and as recently as just two days before the meeting that ended in gunfire. Although Garcia was facing a number of issues, both personally and professionally, he gave no indication to Woo or Kozak that he was targeting Kozak for an attack.

This parallels workplace violence and assassination research from the US Secret Service's 1998 study on "Protective Intelligence and Threat Assessment Investigations," as part of its "Exceptional Case Study Project," written by USSS psychologist Dr. Robert Fein and USSS Supervisory Special Agent Bryan Vossekuil. Perpetrators who want to carry out their attacks don't warn the target directly. If they do make threats, they are said to a third-party, like a family member, a friend, or a co-worker. There is no evidence that Garcia voiced any threats to his colleagues about shooting Kevin Kozak.

Further, in cases of "blue on blue violence," where a law enforcement officer plans to kill other armed colleagues, there is often extraordinary vigilance on the part of the perpetrator not to reveal any part of his plan, so as not to be stopped. Just like law enforcement officers don't usually warn their family or co-workers prior to their suicides, workplace violence perpetrators who happen to be cops know they can be foiled if they discuss their plans. (Police suicides are more common than we like to believe: over 140 per year, which asks the disturbing question, "How many police suicides could have actually started as a workplace violence incident at the police station?")

Just two days before the shooting – Valentine's Day – Woo had spent several hours in his office with Garcia, offering him support and giving him options for his career. He gave no warning signs to Woo about his intentions, in fact, both left the office at 7:30 pm and ended their meeting with a friendly handshake.

Woo asked Kozak to help with a coaching meeting with Garcia on February 16th. While seated in front of Kozak's desk, a verbal confrontation quickly erupted between Kozak and Garcia. Garcia quickly pulled out his service semi-auto handgun from his waistband holster and fired multiple rounds at Kozak, striking him in the arms, legs, and torso. Woo immediately wrestled with Garcia for control of his handgun but he continued shooting erratically at Kozak. Woo gained control of the barrel of Garcia's handgun and told Garcia to stop, but Garcia muttered, "It's too late" and attempted to grab Woo's holstered handgun.

Woo defended his weapon and as a last resort, fired on Garcia, ending the threat to him and his boss.

"I reverted to my training," he said. "I holstered my weapon, secured Garcia's handgun, and rendered first-aid to Mr. Kozak by wrapping his injured hand and back with gym clothing lying nearby. Then I opened the office door so first responders could help."

The Long Beach, CA Police Department, along with Los Angeles Police officers and HSI agents already inside the building, responded to the scene. As soon as medical and police help arrived, Woo said he relinquished scene command, knowing he was in a crime scene, and went into an adjoining conference room to prepare himself for post-critical incident procedures. His entry into the difficult world of an officer-involved shooting began.

The FBI and the U.S. Attorney's Office investigated the shooting, classifying it as an incident of workplace violence. After a year-long inquiry, they cleared Woo in the incident, saying his actions were justified based on the dangerousness of Garcia's actions toward Kozak and himself.

Kozak continues to recover from his gunshot wounds, as does Woo, who injured his shoulder and tore ligaments in his knee during his fight with Garcia. "I drew my firearm when Garcia failed to surrender his handgun – clearly he was not going to stop. I was not going to die that day and I was not going to let Mr. Kozak die that day either."

Agent Woo says as a result of his continuing post-traumatic stress about the incident he still has some symptoms and is saddened anytime a mass shooting erupts, being reminded of what happened based on seeing people, items, or places associated with his incident.

Woo credits his family, friends, his therapists, HSI leadership, and his police colleagues for their continuing emotional support. He said that one of the factors in his shooting that served as an obstacle to his recovery was the relentless media coverage of the event, especially in southern California. While he understood that the media had its job to do, in this era of nonstop coverage and critiques of events where they have little information and few of the facts, their immediate assessment was often harsh, one-sided, or plain wrong.

The influence of social media was a factor in his case as well, where the public, and people inside DHS in general and HSI, in particular, made a number of comments on Internet sites. This barrage of both positive and negative feedback in these types of events can interfere with survivors' abilities to cope with the trauma of their situations.

He said, "Some people blogged that I either shot too soon or not soon enough. The reality was that I tried to save both of them and it was hand-to-hand combat to the death. I dealt with a deadly situation that I didn't cause, and I was forced to shoot a fellow special agent in order to save another special agent, which ultimately prevented further deaths in the office."

Perry Woo has served a long career with the US Customs and DHS. As a survivor of a critical incident, a psychologically traumatic event, and a workplace violence shooting involving a fellow special agent he knew, Woo feels he was in a unique position to write policy and provide assistance and support to other agents for his agency, DHS, and other federal law enforcement agencies.

He was active in his agency's programs in workplace violence, peer support, critical incident planning, effective media management, and the treatment and care for agents who have been in shootings.

The events of February 16, 2012, at the Long Beach, CA federal building were both horrific and unique. While incidents of workplace violence involving current or former employees make the news with alarming frequency today, those involving law enforcement officers are still quite rare. But the impact of that day will affect Perry Woo and Kevin Kozak for the rest of their lives.

NOTE: The views in this article do not necessarily represent the views or policy of DHS, Immigration and Customs Enforcement (ICE), HSI, or any part of the Federal government.

CHAPTER 28

HOW PREPARED ARE YOU AT HOME, IN THE CAR, AND OUT AND ABOUT?

You had a full day at work. You've just finished that heaping bowl of ice cream after a way-too-filling dinner and are about to fall into the recliner and enjoy an evening of TV. Your attempts to fight off sleep are not helped by your wife already dozing away on her couch and the cat snoring, snuggled across you in the Lazy Boy. You decide not to fight it, to just accept the relaxation, and you don't even realize you're asleep until you're awakened by the cat leaping off you and your wife's hand on your foot. There's an upset look on her face and she is saying, "What was that?" Fighting off the fog of sleep, you realize the shaking sound at your front door is someone trying to pry his way into your house. What do you do now?

You had a full day and a half at work. It's dark, you're

hungry, and as you pull into the driveway, the automatic garage door seemingly takes way too long to open. Finally, the door opens and you pull in, careful not to hit the bikes and other garage mess. Reminder to self to change that burned out garage door light bulb. You stop the engine, unbuckle, and open the door. Grabbing your stuff, you hear footsteps behind you. You see two people standing at the opening of your garage. What do you do now?

You have a shopping cart full of essentials from your weekly trip to Walmart. Grabbing your keys, you unlock your Jeep, open the back, and begin the proper staging of the essentials to avoid having them fall about while you're driving home. Squatting down, you grab the case of water from the bottom of the cart and, looking up, you notice a guy walking deliberately towards you with his hands inside his jacket. He looks around as if he is checking to see if anyone is watching. He starts to pull something out of his jacket as he nears you. What do you do now?

All of us have daily routines that have us at home, using transportation, and going out and about. Have you considered these possible "what ifs," and what would you do if those "what ifs" really occurred? Have you ever sat down to consider each part of your routine and what you might face if someone violated it? Have you thought about what you would do to protect yourself or your loved ones?

Does this scenario sound more familiar to you? You arrive home from a long day at work. You are a legally-armed citizen and when you come home you are met by your spouse, kids, pets, and whoever may be visiting. You have your favorite spot to drop off your keys, sunglasses, wallet, hat, knife, and pocket change. You quickly wash up because the faster you get into the kitchen the quicker the hunger pangs will be silenced. Because you have kids, you place your weapon in its lockbox in the bedroom and hit the kitchen. This routine is based upon the presupposition that nothing has ever happened, day in and day out, and this routine has safely ended every one of your armed days without harm to you or your family. But, are you still safe, and is this routine adequate?

With very few exceptions every post-interview to a violent incident has included statements like: "I sensed something was wrong," "I didn't think it would ever happen to us," "I always had my weapon locked up and secured from my kids," "It happened so fast," "I saw them but didn't think they would do anything like this."

Bad things do happen and being unprepared rarely helps you out of a bad situation. One essential to being a legally-armed citizen and Carrying Concealed is being prepared throughout your daily routine. Sadly, as with every routine, complacency can be a large kink in your perceived armor of self-protection and safety. Taking the time to consider your routine paths and usual stops can be a lifesaver from future surprises. Let's take a second look at the examples noted above.

While you, your spouse, and your cat are sleeping after a long hard day and a great dinner, a threat may be right outside your home. Your worst situation is to be awakened by someone breaking in. However, the best course is to have the offender not choose to target your house or to attempt to break into your sanctuary in the first place. Even though you are legally armed and have most every right to protect your family and property, getting ahead of the threat is the best first course of your self-defense. Have you ever stood outside your house in a place a burglar or other felon might stand in determining which house to break into? Do you have a well-lit outside perimeter with motion detection lights? Do you have security screen doors and strong deadbolts that can withstand forced break-ins? Do you use locks on your exterior doors, windows, and gates? Do you have an alarm system with posted signs saying as much? The ideal situation is to have a hardened residence that any nefarious offender would consider too risky or troublesome to breach.

As you remain inside the house comfortably, are you aware if someone gets near your house before he/she gets to the front door? Ring, Canary, and other area motion sensors with lights and cameras will provide you with early detection of activities in the approach areas and entry zones to your residence. Supported by proper lighting, early detection allows you to get advanced notice of potential threats, allowing you to take practiced safety actions inside your house.

The first three paragraphs of this chapter end with the question: What do you do now? The key to this chapter is to not ever put yourself in a position where you have to immediately and spontaneously consider what to do now. Practicing our Three As (Awareness, Avoidance, and Action), aligned with hardening our daily routines, will prevent shock-and-awe if an attacker targets us.

We are all aware that home break-ins, burglaries, and invasions from multiple suspects can happen. We are also aware that criminals will target our routines, such as when we are parking our cars in the garage, running errands at shopping centers, and stopping at coffee shops.

Having a strong sense of Awareness extends your safety zones and removes the shades of denial that bad things only happen to other people. We already know that criminals most often target the unaware, the complacent, and the easy prey.

Avoidance allows us to act on the early signs and indicators of threats, based upon our heightened awareness. We know criminals use darkness to hide like the cockroaches they are. So, we prevent them from having such convenience by installing motion detection lights, working garage opener lights, and yard perimeter lights. Having lights removes the offender's edge. Another way to Avoid threatening issues and situations at home might include immediately shutting your garage door once you pull in. Awareness and Avoidance in a shopping center parking lot could start with where you park, how you look around when you're in the lot, and early defensive action when you see a nefarious person moving toward you.

Another aspect of Avoidance is not being caught unprepared and without your weapon. If you are aware that you could be attacked in your house, store, parking lot, and garage, then you must avoid being caught not having your weapon or not having fast access to your weapon in these places. In your home, you should have the means to acquire your weapon safely in those rooms or entry/exit points where you could be targeted. We all understand you MUST ensure all firearms are not accessible to children, guests, or strangers, but you must also have the means to get your hands on your gun if you need it. (This usually means you need several gun safes, in several parts of your house, not just the one in your bedroom closet.) A big part of avoidance is ensuring you are not caught unprepared or without your gear.

It's worth repeating that when Awareness and Avoidance fail, you must be able to Act decisively with practiced purpose to save yourself and your family. If you're unable to avoid the threat, then you must have practiced and be mentally prepared to use your legal right to defend yourself. To be able to act decisively in a time of need requires practicing the possible situations as they match your life routines. Where and how you store your weapon in your home is based upon understanding the likely threat situations you may face - and the people you live with - to include their security considerations.

Often people who are trained to be legally armed citizens and join the Concealed Carry lifestyle do not take the time to understand when they are vulnerable in their routines or seemingly safe spaces. Any person can make the choice to carry, but one responsibility of Carrying Concealed is possessing a deeper level of knowledge of threats and preparations to deal with those threats. The process of Carrying Concealed and being legally armed requires strong core competencies and foundational understanding of potential threats. If you can avoid the gun battle, you will be better off. But if a gun battle is called for, you had better be fully prepared.

Central to your core and foundational responsibility is to understand your routines, have a strong awareness of each of the spaces you will occupy, seek to deny, deter, or avoid all threats, and if needed act with practiced decisiveness. Take the time and assess your daily routines by asking: "What could happen here?" "Knowing what I know could happen, how should I avoid situations that put me and my family at risk?" and "If I need to act, what are my best steps to protect myself and them?"

Ensure that you match your gear to the expected situations and have that gear staged, ready, and able to perform. Finally, ensure you are as ready as possible to act when situations come knocking and avoid having to wonder, "What do I do now?"

How prepared are you at home, in the car, and out and about? You should ask yourself this question several times each day. The criminal will try to determine his chance of exploiting you at his desired location, based upon his assessment of your readiness. The legal system will determine through an investigation of what steps you took to be aware and to avoid a bad situation. Therefore, the best person to be asking this question about you is you, to put yourself ahead of threat situations and bad outcomes.

AFTERWORD(S)

"Happiness Is a Warm Gun." – The Beatles, The White Album, 1968

"Under pressure, you don't rise to the occasion; you sink to the level of your training. That's why we train so hard." – US Navy SEALS

"A man reaches a certain age where he doesn't want any drama. He doesn't want to fight anyone – and if forced to, he will not fight fair. He will not quit and there are no weapons he will not use. It's best to leave him alone with his coffee, bourbon, and cigars. Don't poke the old men. They will hurt you."

-- Quoted by some awesome people on various places on Twitter and Facebook

ABOUT THE AUTHORS

STEVE ALBRECHT

Steve is a Colorado-based HR trainer and security consultant.

He worked for the San Diego Police Department from 1984 to 1999, both as a full-time officer and later as a reserve sergeant and a Domestic Violence Unit investigator. He has written 18 other books, including ***Ticking Bombs*** (1994), one of the first business books on workplace violence prevention. His six police tactical books include ***Contact & Cover,*** with John Morrison***; Streetwork; Surviving Street Patrol; One-Strike Stopping Power; Tactical Perfection for Street Cops;*** and ***Patrol Cop.***

Order the first book in this series, ***Albrecht on Guns: Tactical Concealed Carry, Volume 1*** at Amazon at https://amzn.to/2LJQfXA

Please visit www.DrSteveAlbrecht.com/orders/ to order copies of Steve's other books.

MICHAEL FARROW

Michael is the Northern Arizona-based CEO of PIC Alliance LLC

As Founder and CEO, Mike lead's PIC Alliance LLC in assisting organizations, private security, and law enforcement protective efforts overcome the many challenges of establishing protective intelligence concepts and operations.

Mike's career started with serving the nation as a Pararescueman with the U.S. Air Force. After transitioning from the military, Mike began a 32-year career with an aerospace company, advancing to a senior-level management position focusing on corporate and government security.

During his tenure Mike has operated in over 27 countries, supporting protective services, integrated security solutions, and situational awareness platforms for local, state, federal, and international government programs.

Mike holds a Master's Degree in Strategic Intelligence and a Master's Degree in Management. He has received multiple awards from local and state governments during his decades of service to law enforcement and first-responders.

From his days as a Boy Scout-Eagle Scout to his time saving lives as an Air Force-Pararescueman, Mike's focus has always been on helping others. He believes through his personal protective service experiences he is able to recognize the need for enhanced tools and applications for getting ahead and inside the threat curve to protect others.

www.ingramcontent.com/pod-product-compliance
Lightning Source LLC
LaVergne TN
LVHW010655110826
845149LV00014B/3106

* 9 7 8 1 9 6 0 4 9 9 9 0 5 *